The Artistry *of* Handwork

The Artistry *of* Handwork

Jaya Jaitly

NIYOGI BOOKS

Cover pic:

Coloured bamboo birds used to embellish baskets. This picture has been chosen for the sheer simplicity and artistic elegance of the birds, and because this craft is practised by one of the poorest and most marginalised communities in Uttar Pradesh.

Published by

NIYOGI BOOKS

D-78, Okhla Industrial Area, Phase-I
New Delhi-110 020, INDIA
Tel: 91-11-26816301, 49327000
Fax: 91-11-26810483, 26813830
email: niyogibooks@gmail.com
website: www.niyogibooksindia.com

Text : Jaya Jaitly
Design: Diya Dasgupta

ISBN: 978-93-83098-18-7
Publication: 2014

Printed at: Niyogi Offset Pvt. Ltd., New Delhi, India

Dedication

This book is dedicated to artisans everywhere for whom handwork is worship, creative expression and earnings.

It is a collection of random images that are not meant to inform or educate but to give the viewer joy at the sight of the simple beauty of handwork. The practitioners of these crafts are anonymous. However, each pursues a dream to excel and find happiness through art.

The Philosophy of Handwork

In a quiet corner of Hakone, a weekend resort in Japan, is the Pal-Shimonaka Memorial dedicated to friendship between India and Japan. Yasaburo Shimonaka began life as a potter, and went through life as a philanthropist and a widely respected leader of the publishing world. Dr Radhabinod Pal represented India as a judge on the Far East International Military Tribunal. A firm believer in Vedanta, he resolutely upheld the integrity of the law. Along with Shimonaka he did much to bring to bear on Japan the teachings of Gandhi. So influenced was Shimonaka that, at the age of eighty, he went back to making pottery, believing that this was one of the ways to re-establish 'the Dignity of the Eastern Mind'.

The very basis for any philosophy has to be a moral one, quite unlike propositions that, while offering a framework of intellectual arguments, does little to raise the moral and spiritual condition of man. The value and assets accorded to handwork, at best, has been placed on a lower scale than most other economic activities and, at worst, been relegated to a sectional position within the 'also ran' economic alternatives of the past five decades. Yet, if we look back a little and observe the panorama over which it presides and the range of luminaries who have subscribed to this philosophy, whether their immediate concern was economic, social, aesthetic or spiritual, we will find that handwork is one of the most potent outer manifestations of a composite philosophy. Thus the simple charkha (spinning wheel) became the single most powerful symbol of the freedom struggle in India.

The motif of Gandhi's philosophy was that 'the supreme consideration is man'. This did not mean the individual, egocentric, self-centred man, but the single thread of consciousness that links man's activities with the Creator, who is, after all, a creation of the mind. If one sees a craftsperson at work one will see this very process in operation. The spiritual process is a linking of the highly individual inner self to the movements of the hand, then on to the needs of the community and the larger web of society, finally to connect with the world and the cosmos.

What is paradoxical about the creation of community products through the hand skills of individuals is the manner in which the craftsperson places the creativity of the entire self into community art – that is, into activity that results in the effacement of the self. There are no gimmicks or personalised specialties or even flourishes of signature. Painting of religious themes on walls or on cloth was always considered a mode of worship. In India, craft is a community industry performed for community service, and the intention is for its wide use rather than its wide appreciation, or the specific recognition of the individual maker. And yet, each is a piece unto itself – the creation of a unique pair of hands.

Gandhi believed in the indivisibility of truth; therefore, to injure or exploit another was akin to doing violence to one's soul. The economic implication of this is that it is morally necessary to provide sufficient work for everyone to be able to feed and clothe oneself and the family. For everyone to be provided with work that maintains the dignity of the human being, it is necessary, according to Gandhi, to place physical labour on par with intellectual labour. Going a step further, he suggested that sound educational practices, namely, the combination of knowledge and handicrafts, or what Plato called 'music and gymnastics', is in effect sound social practice. The sacramental nature of any work through which we identify with the poor, and thereby the whole of mankind, was the philosophy of mankind itself. And the best example of its realisation was the spinning wheel. It sounds simplistic but unless philosophical and moral concepts are rooted to concrete action, they remain just so much hot air. After all, was not the simple gesture of grasping a handful of salt enough to electrify the meaning of freedom from foreign rule?

The steamroller effect of mechanisation and the Industrial Revolution in Britain pauperised the Indian handloom weaver in favour of the textile mills of Manchester and Lancashire. Now, with the second onslaught in the form of multinational corporations and their high-technology methods of production, it is illusory to presume that our illiterate and impoverished craftspeople will have access to skills which would help them to be absorbed into these new workplaces. As for the highly skilled and artistic craftsperson, it can surely be no credit to modern civilisation that he should now have to resort to punching a computerised machine. Machines should obviously assist people in their skills rather than displace them. Here is where Gandhi's philosophy of handwork becomes relevant. He maintained that where the nature of work does not degrade or dehumanise the individual but shows concern for the quality of life of ordinary people, that work should be encouraged.

Theories of industrial production and employment have always presumed that it is the chosen few who own the means of production and it is they who should gain the most profit with the best outlay. The natural corollary of these theories is that if machines had a larger output than man, then man could be dispensed with. Schumacher, the author of *Small is Beautiful*, made acceptable in economic terms the Gandhian belief that man possessed a soul as well as body. He proposed that methods and machines should be sufficiently cheap in order to be available to everyone, applicable on a small scale, and constituent with the creative needs of man. These were important prerequisites to define the true quality of life. He brought the crucial moral question into the understanding of the role of economics, termed it 'metanomics', and concerned himself more with the adverse social consequences of marketing mass produced goods which displaced the jobs of millions. Schumacher even harmonised his economic precepts with Buddhism and linked himself with this universal philosophy that opposed those who considered goods as more important than people and consumption as more important than creative activity. It meant shifting the emphasis from the worker to the product of work, that is, from the human to the sub-human, essentially surrendering to the forces of evil.

Pattern and design are the most salient features of handcrafted articles. They represent three very important aspects of the link between man and nature. The most profound philosophers, scientists and artists study symmetry and mathematics in the patterns of nature. Look at water, leaves, branches or sand – there are immutable laws that govern their designs. Infinitely varied, yet neither chaotic nor individualistic, they reiterate the concept of continuity and community activity as opposed to anarchy. The creative freedom offered within the limitations of raw material and utility is limitless, unlike the monotony of a pattern governed by a mould or machine. Just like the framework of a raga that has to be adhered to while the musician makes innumerable creative forays within it, the 'art of craft' follows this philosophy.

Soetsu Yanagi, the artist-philosopher of Japan, echoes Gandhi when he says:

> Crafts are of and for the great mass of people and are made in great quantity for daily life. Expensive fine crafts

> for the few are not of the true character of craftsmanship, which being for every man are appropriately decorated with the patterns of every man. It is natural that craft objects be associated with patterns that are also, in a true sense, communal (i.e. of the community). Painting today is prized far more than patterns but the time will come again when this position will be reversed, and beauty that transcends the individual will come to be accorded more importance.

When you look at the delicate fish patterns woven on the borders of a sari from Sambalpur in Odisha, or trace the criss-cross textures of a Tripura basket, the harmony of the senses transmitted between the craftsperson as maker, and the client as user, through designs and patterns illustrates the meaning of this 'quality of life'. The silent, almost prayer-like meditative moments during production add to the many-faceted worth of a crafted object.

Crafting, weaving and other forms of artisanship are community activities, which at the same time assert community identities. This is done subconsciously and is related to historical and cultural influences and the social, religious and domestic needs of the community, tribe or even race. Bamboo artefacts for hunting and thickly woven deep-hued dhotis for women who work the land, the finest muslins for feudal courts, pastel silk tones on embroidered shawls as an item of export, votive offerings to propitiate the gods of the forest – all these bear the imprint of a specific design, suited to a specific purpose rooted in time. The several ethnic tribes of nomadic herdsmen spread across Central Asia, down through Kashmir, Rajasthan, the Thar Desert in Pakistan and the Rann of Kutch in Gujarat are examples of identities established through handcrafted objects of daily use. Wooden cots, storage chests, spice boxes and mirror frames have a distinct style of carving, often inlaid with mirrors. Earthenware pots used for water, milk and buttermilk in hot desert areas have common geometric hand-painted designs linking a millennium of regional tradition with influences of Greek and Nordic designs. Embroidery, encrusted with mirrors of varying sizes, defines the wearer's caste, religion and occupation. While the entire group or tribe may wear the same printed, woven or embroidered headgear, it will be an indicator of its distinction from another group.

Today, as the youth turn to the amorphous 'global' design of T-shirts and jeans manufactured in any factory, owned and controlled by proprietors who live elsewhere, dictated by fashion moguls in Paris or New York, any individualisation or group identity based on traditional cultural practices is effaced. Can the Rajasthani musician sing of his desert in a shining lurex vest and polyester shirt, and does he now have to compete with the flashing images of MTV to be part of the great global culture? At best these folk entertainers, attired in tradition, with their handmade musical instruments and lovingly embroidered leather footwear, will become anthropological amusements at restaurants and festivals for the urban rich, while our young researchers and photographers document them for posterity. At worst, they wallow and degenerate into an orphaned cultural expression with no aesthetic merit. Will our handicrafts, as symbols of a way of life, end up like an exquisite ship in a glass bottle on the mantelpieces of coming generations while seminars on 'ethnicity' and 'identity' are held in air-conditioned conference rooms?

Man's mind creates concepts and his hands create objects. Handwork, handcraft, hand skills, call it what you will, is the reflection of the cosmos in all its manifestations and so becomes one of the nodal points of man's cultural and spiritual expression. The West overran it, and the Far East is fast losing it. We in India, poised precariously between both these cultures and civilisations, have a living philosophy of handwork that we can either preserve or throw away. To preserve it would mean to honour Soetsu Yanagi's dream – to re-establish 'the Dignity of the Eastern Mind'.

~ Jaya Jaitly

In India, everything is hand wrought, and everything, down to the cheapest toy or earthen vessel, is therefore more or less a work of art …The spirit of fine art is everywhere latent in India.

~ C.G.M. Birdwood
The Arts of India

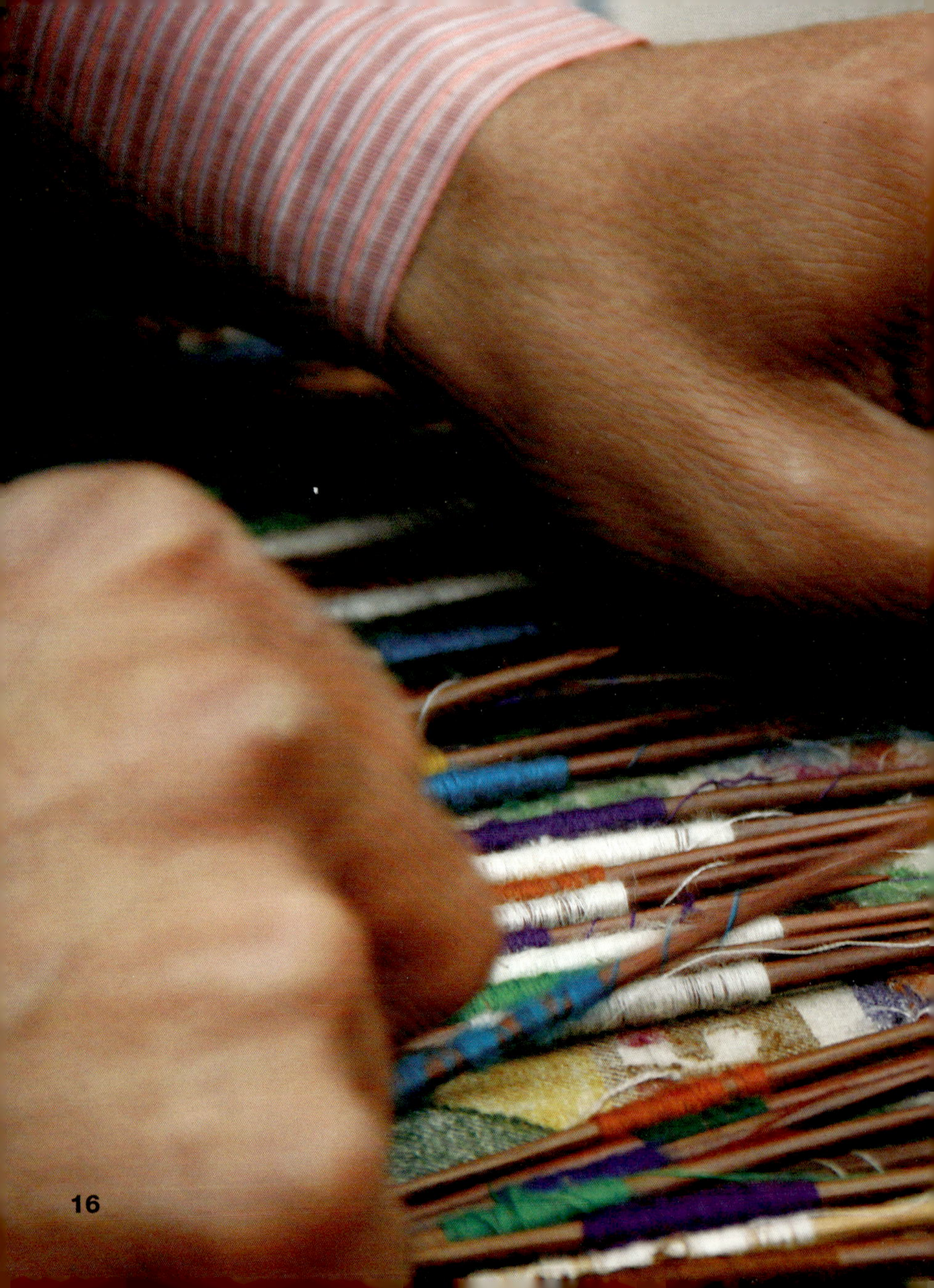

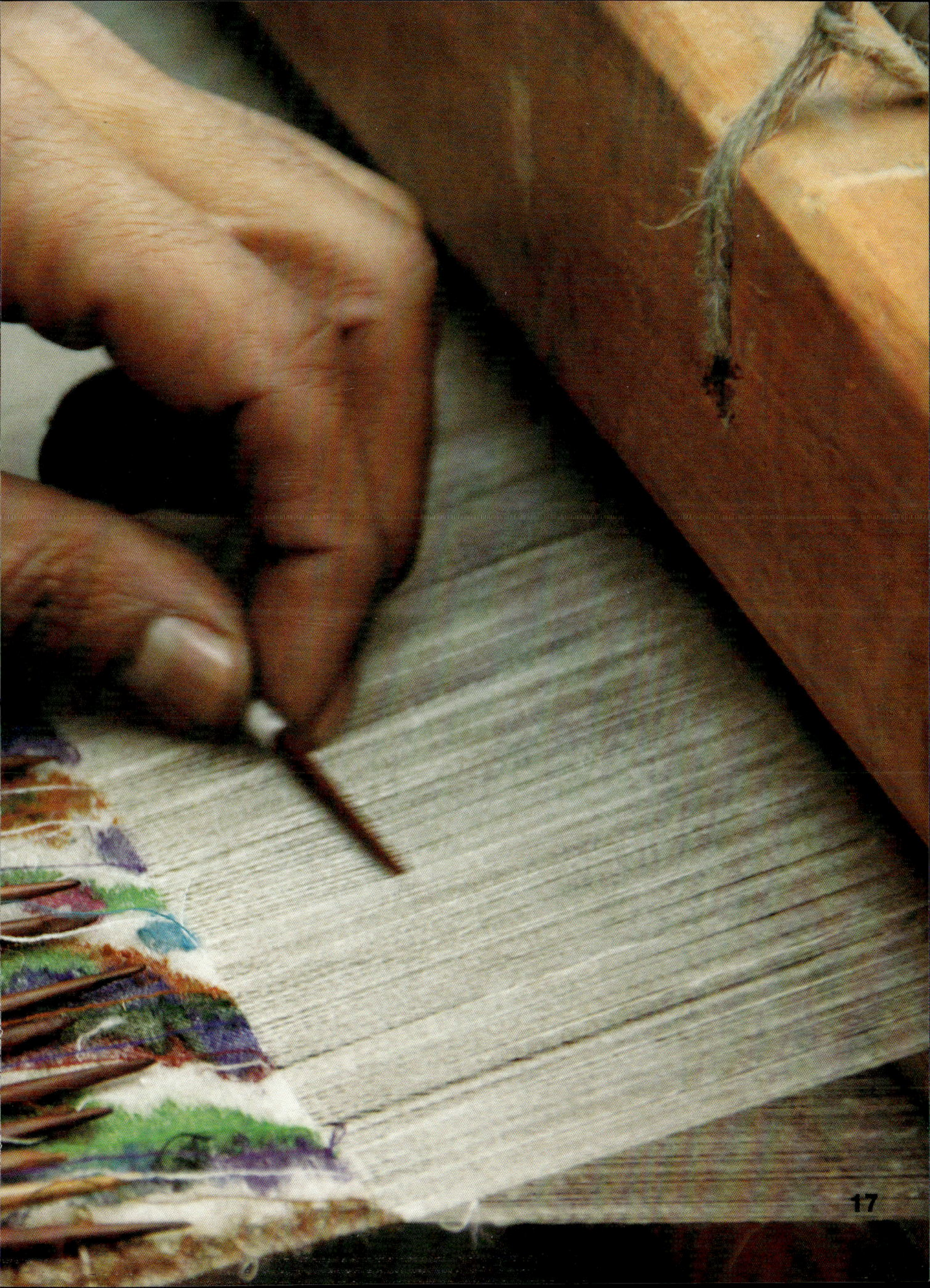

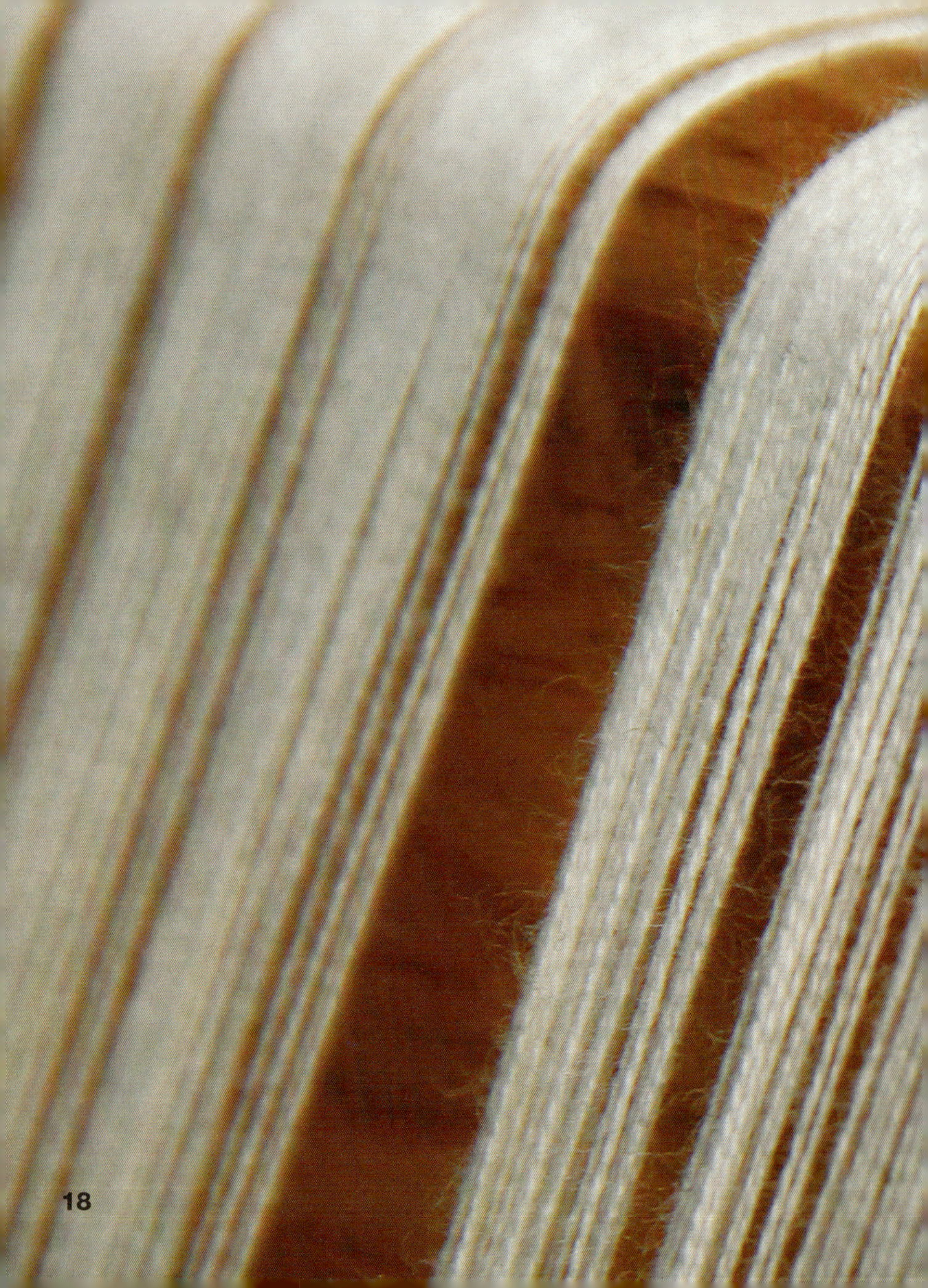

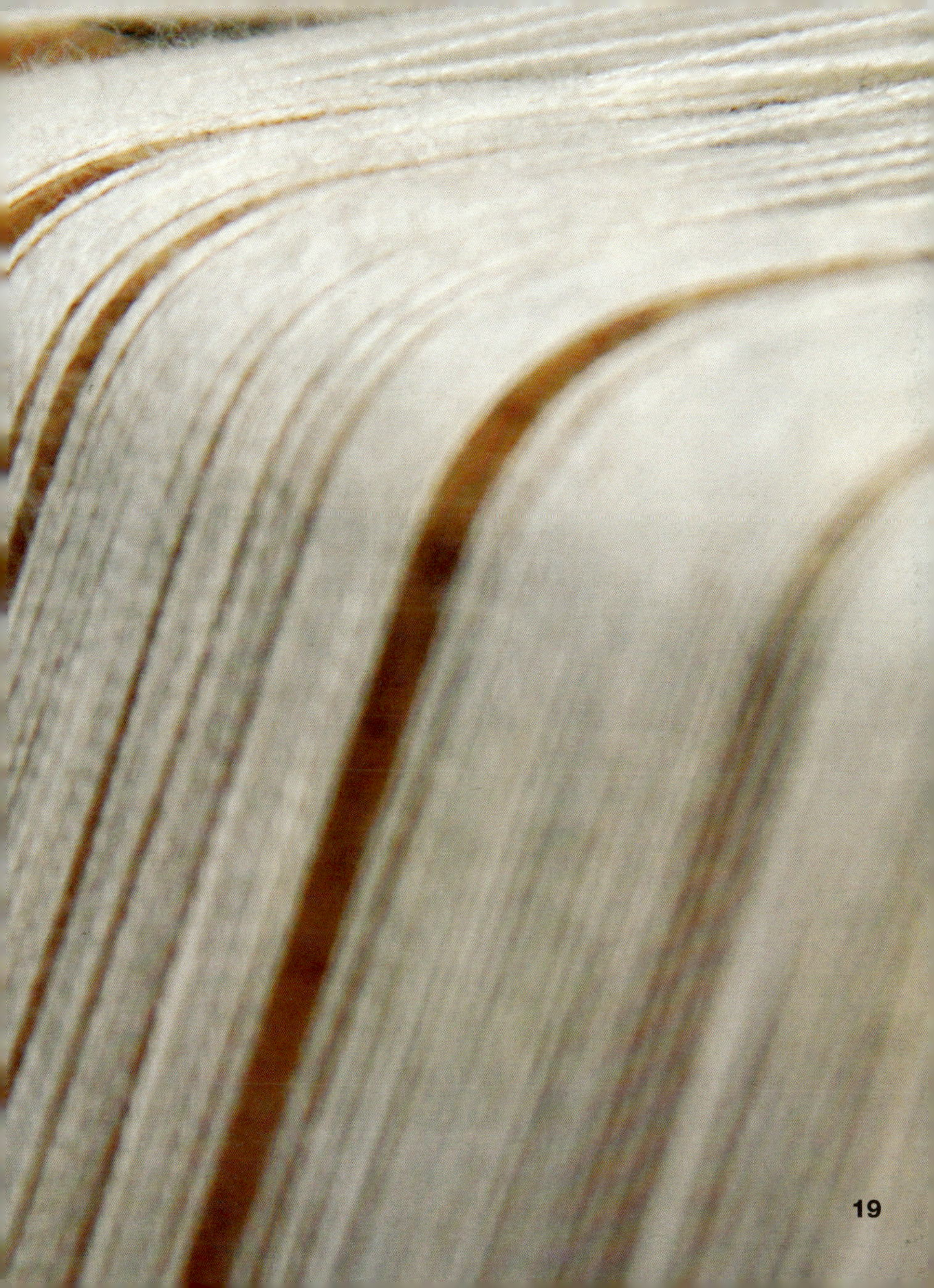

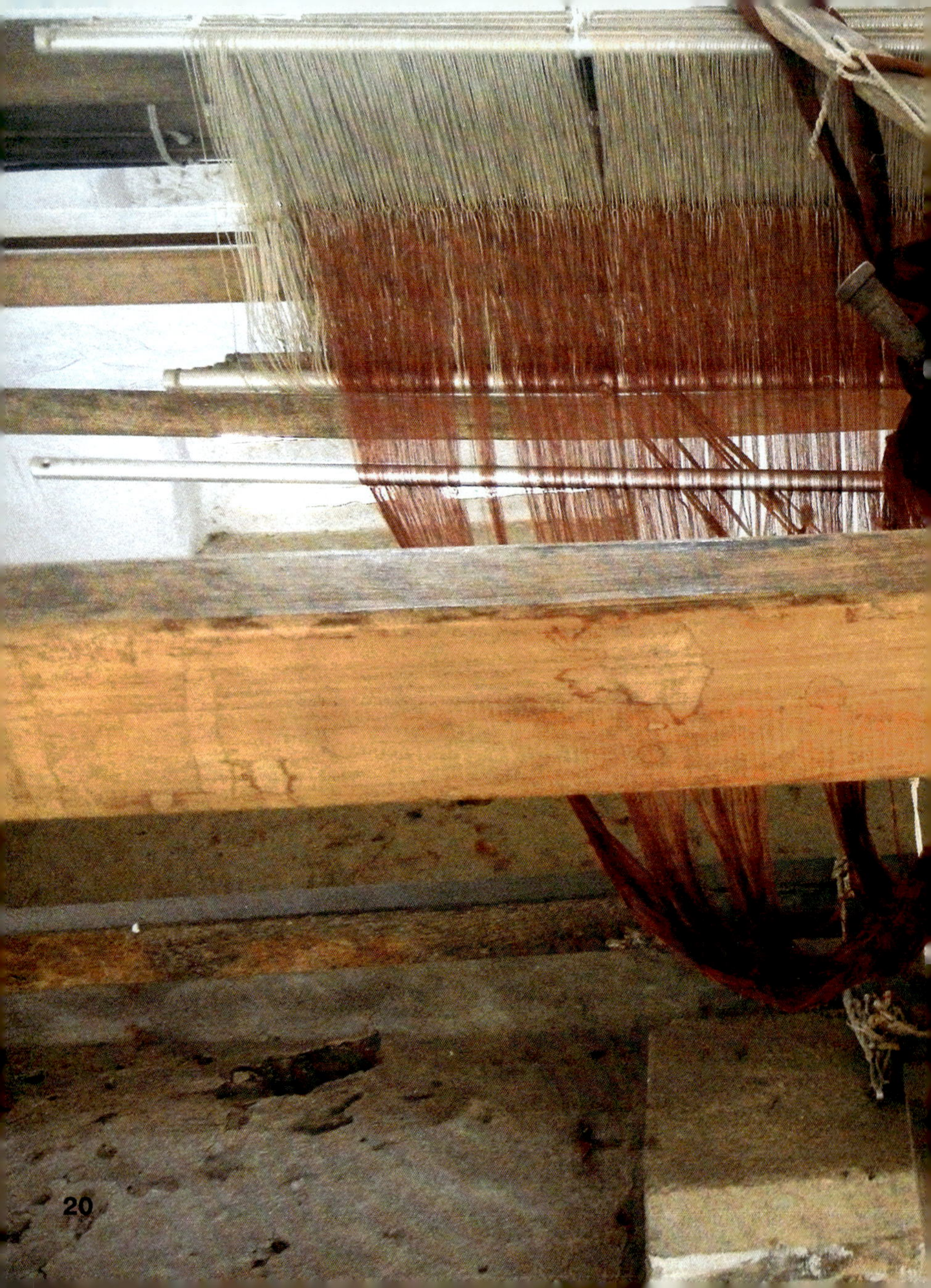

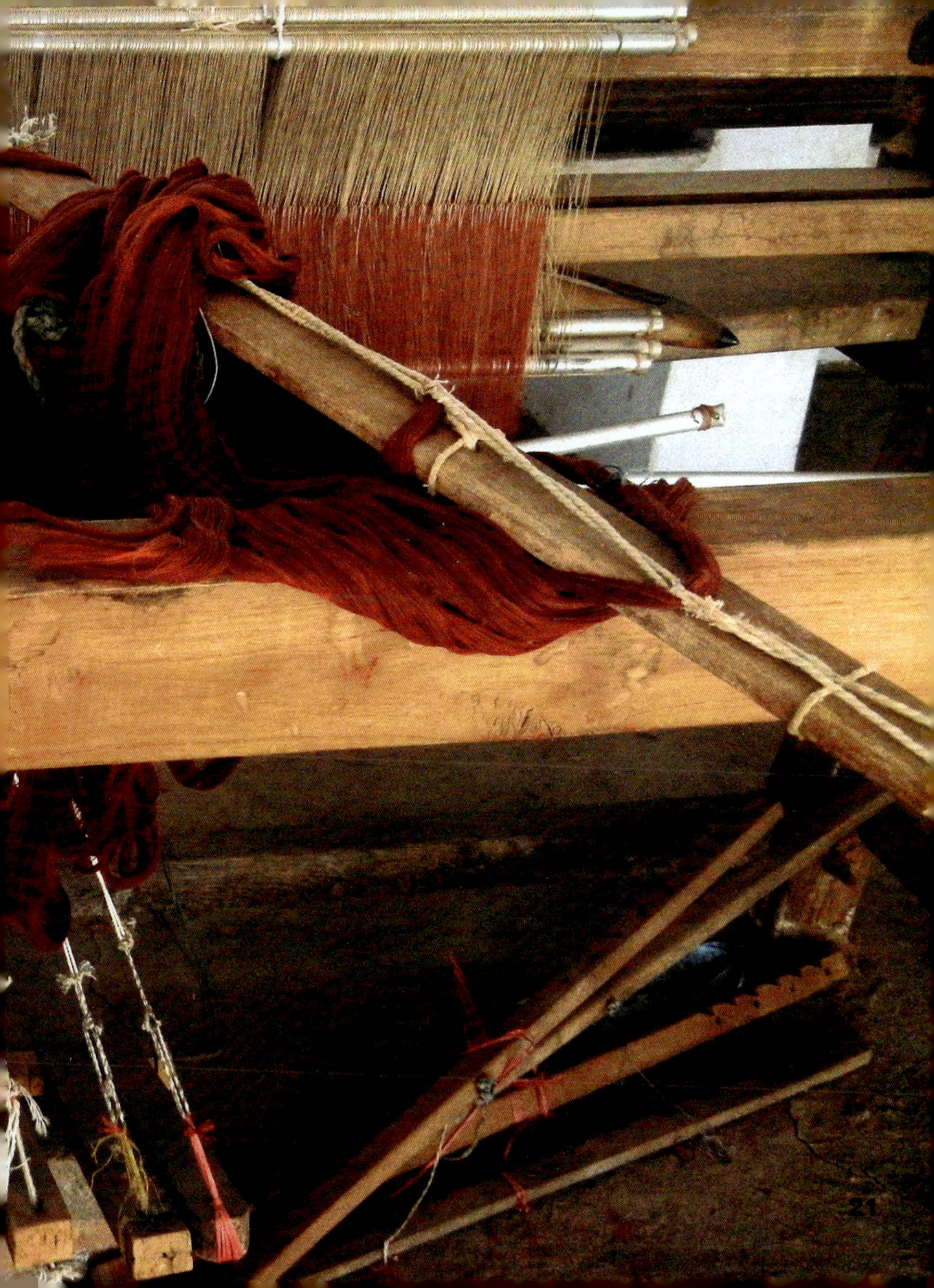

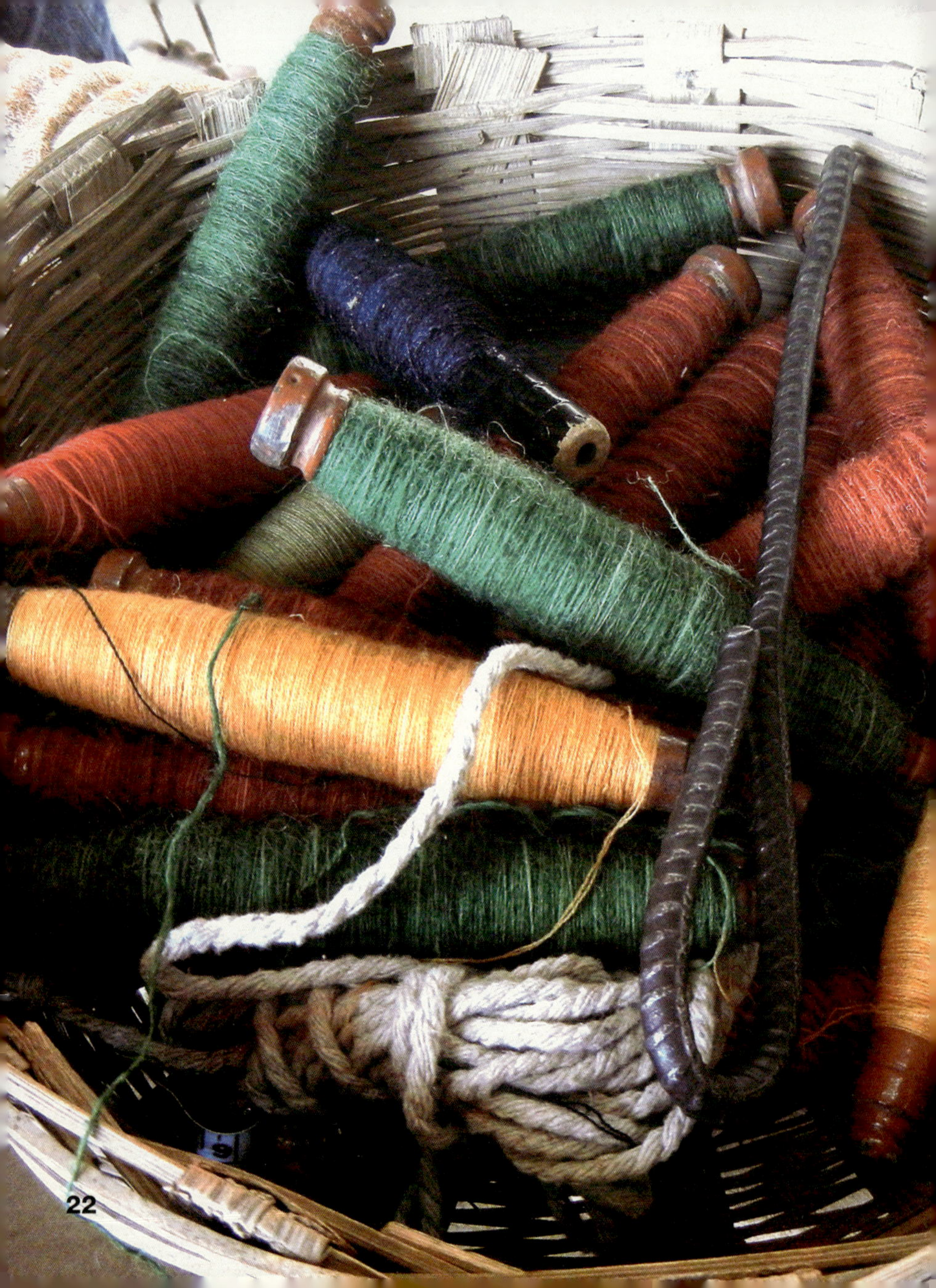

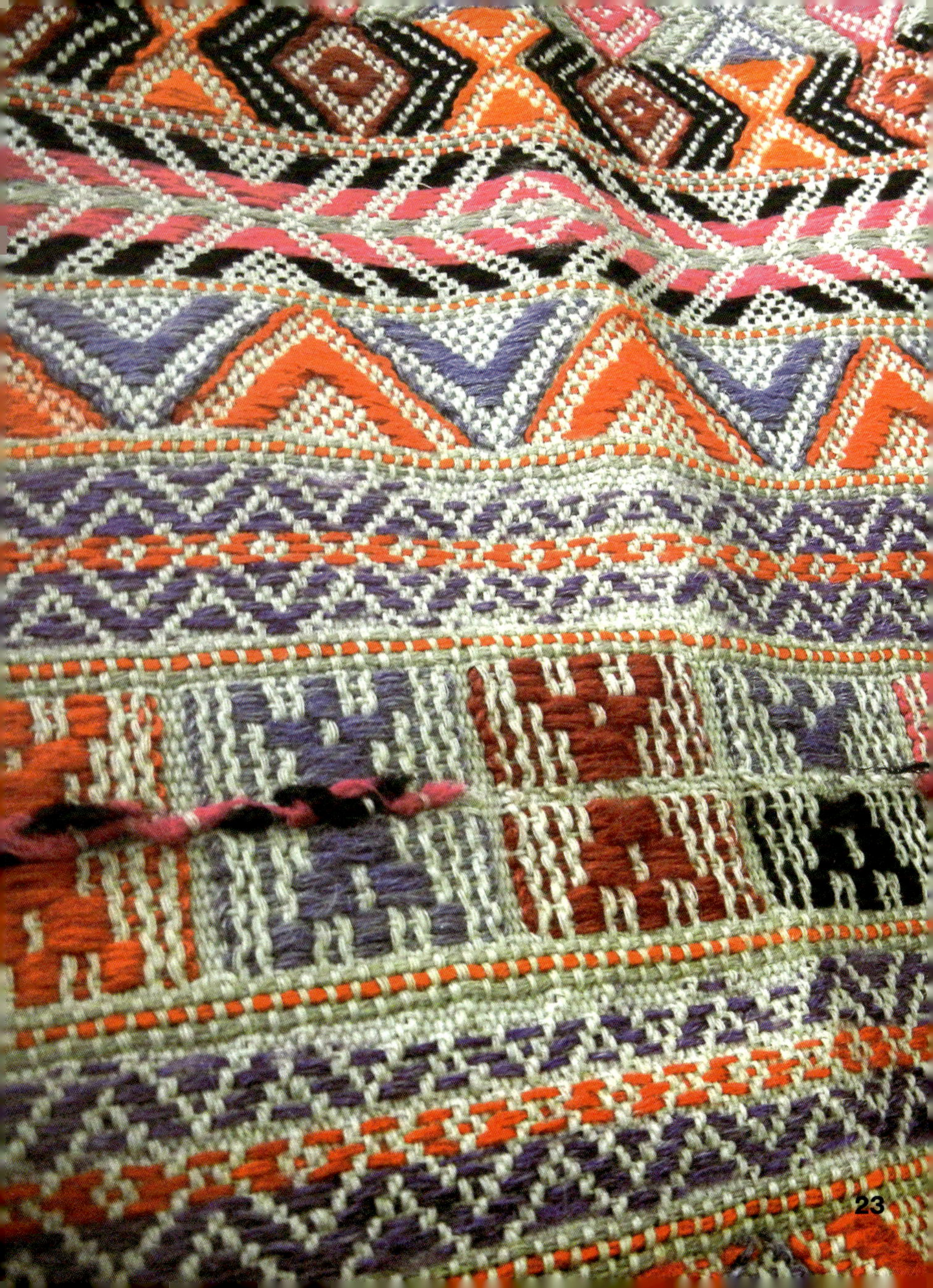

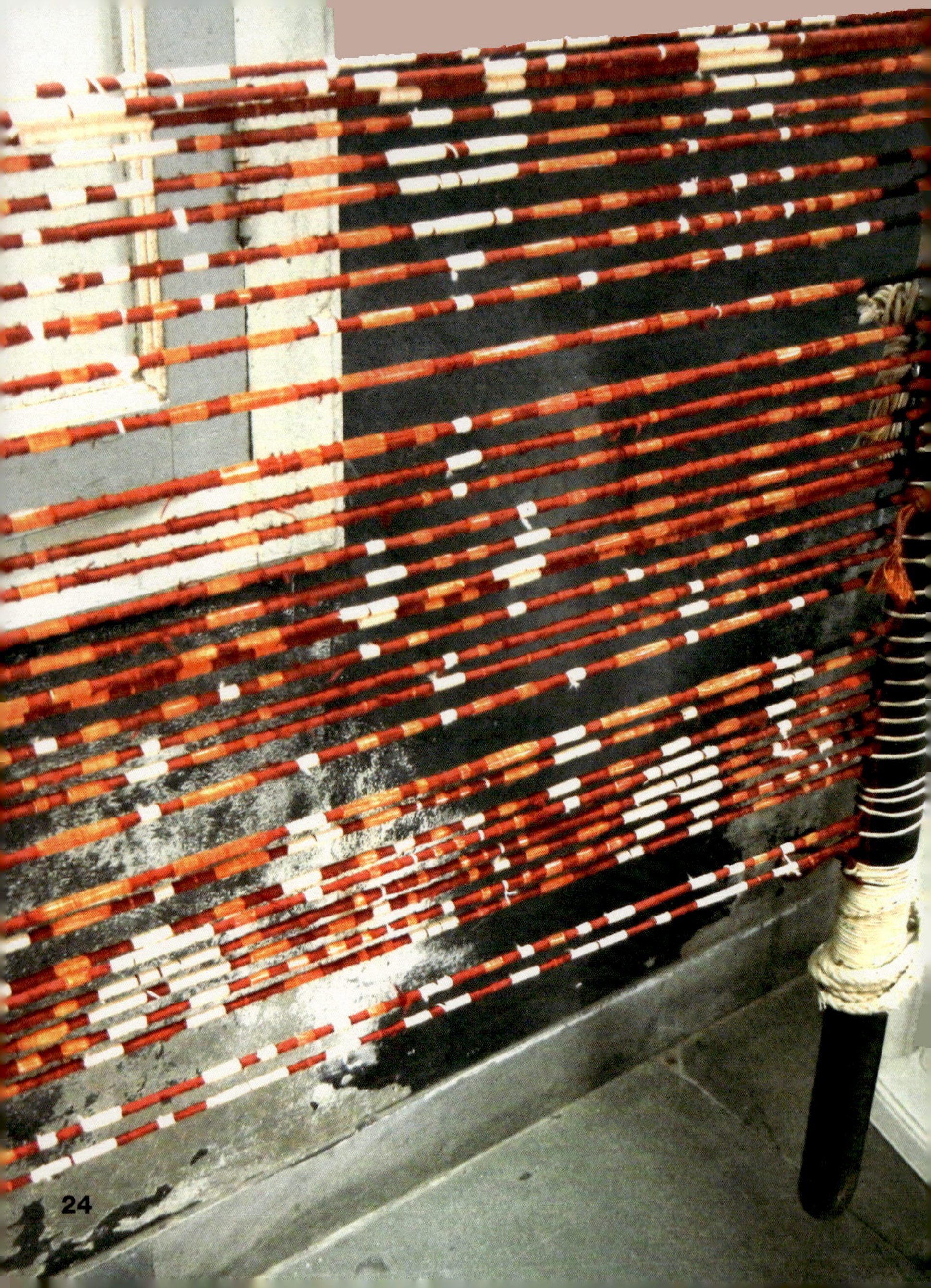

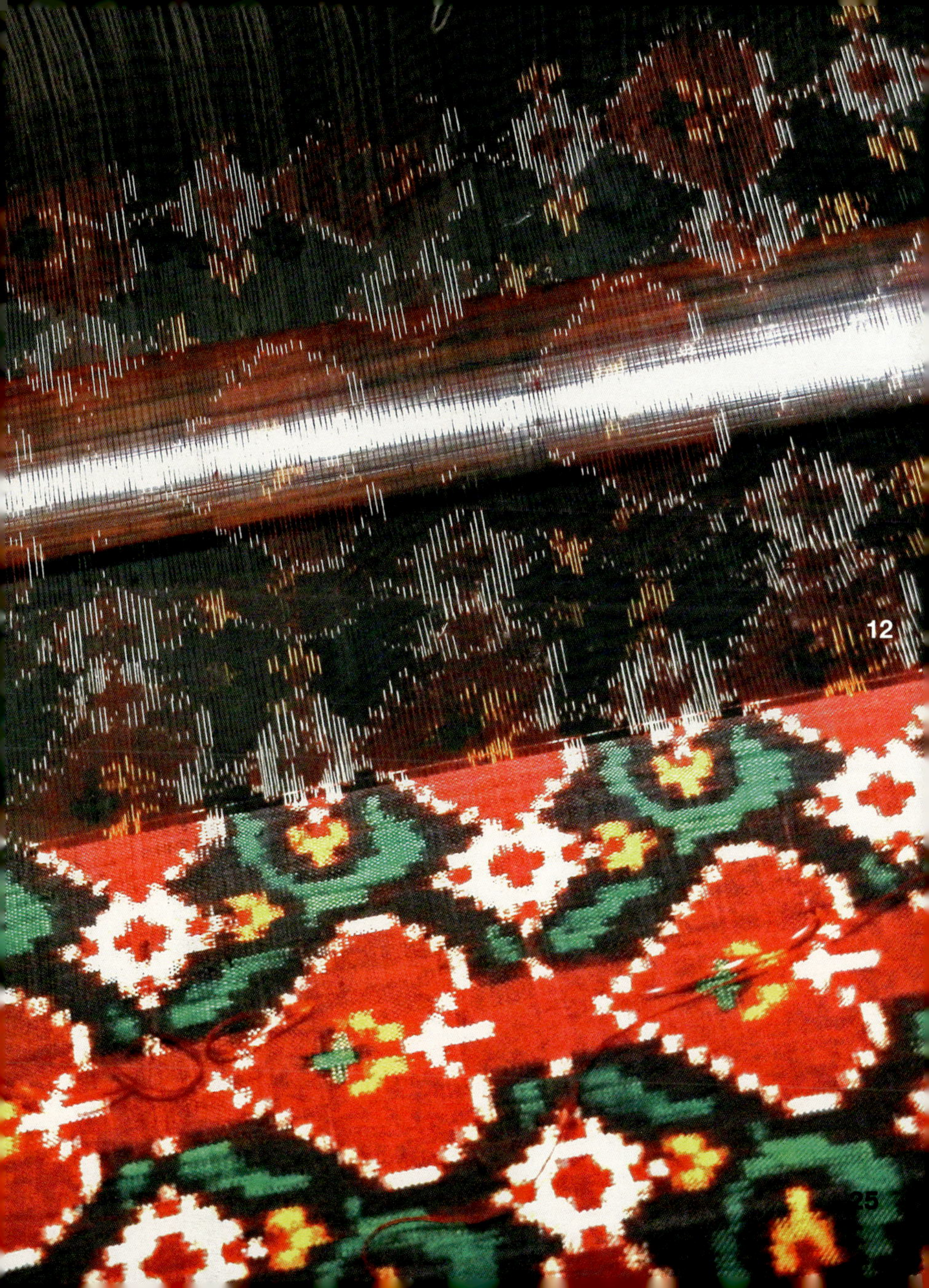

12

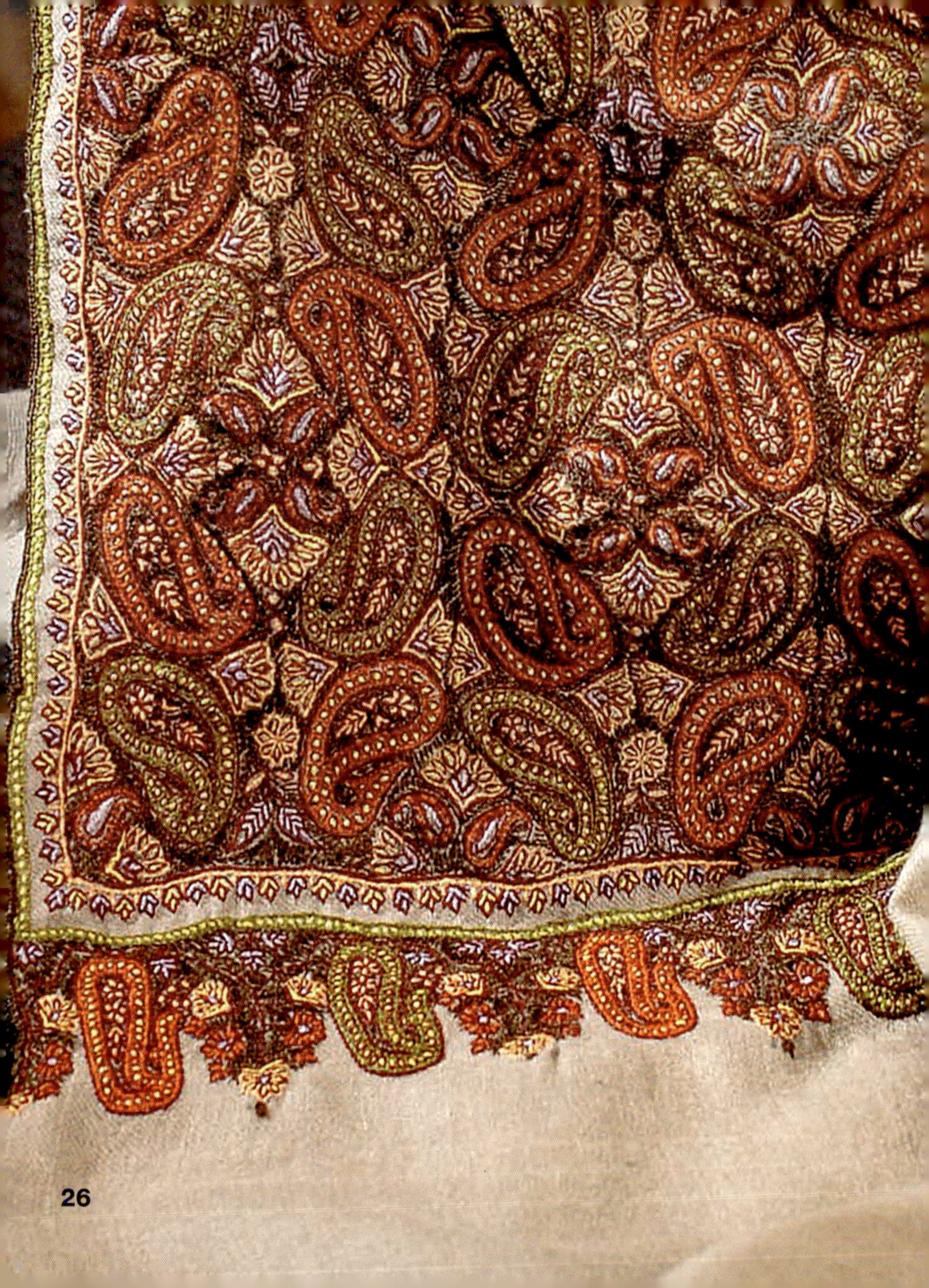

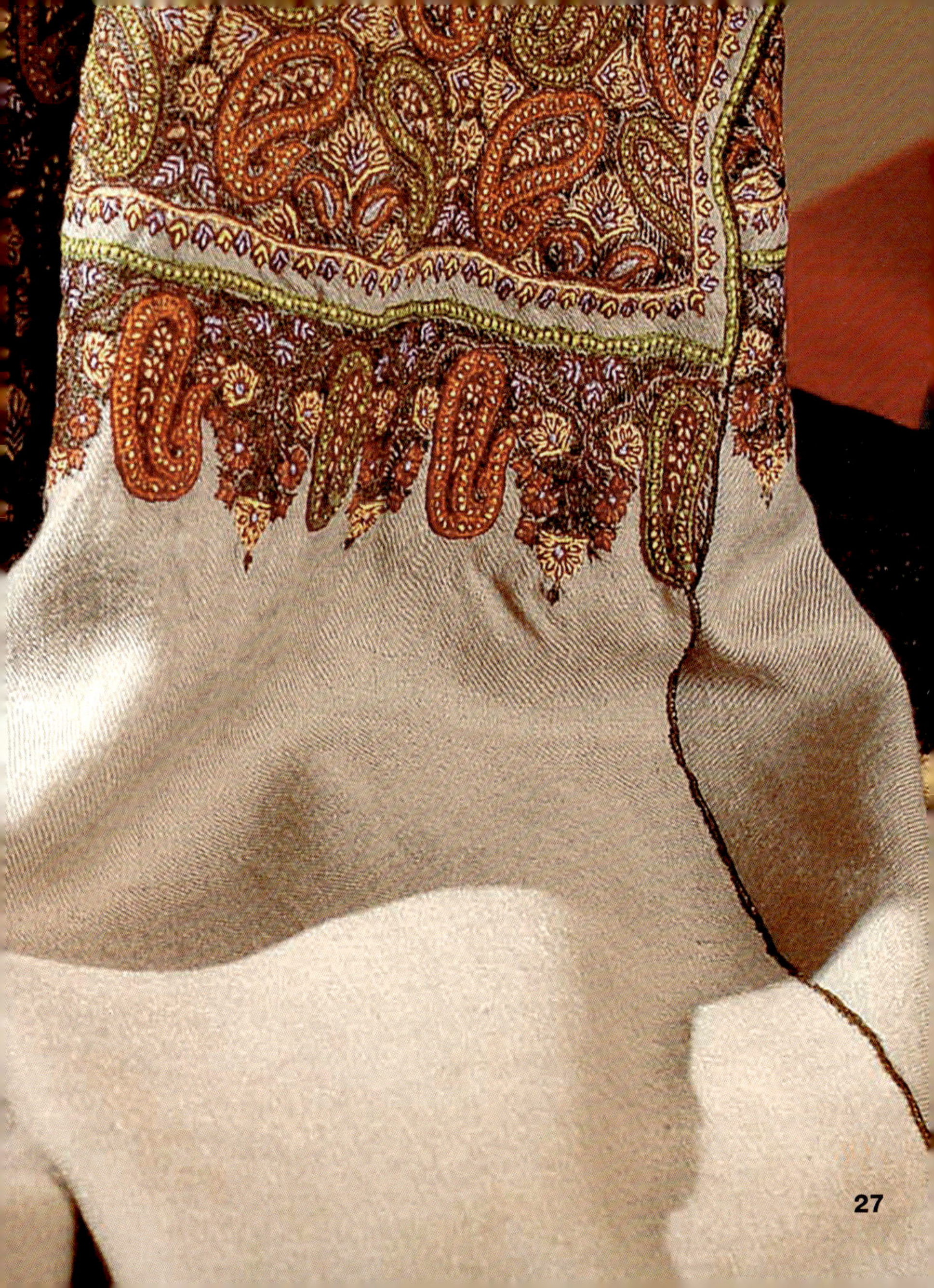

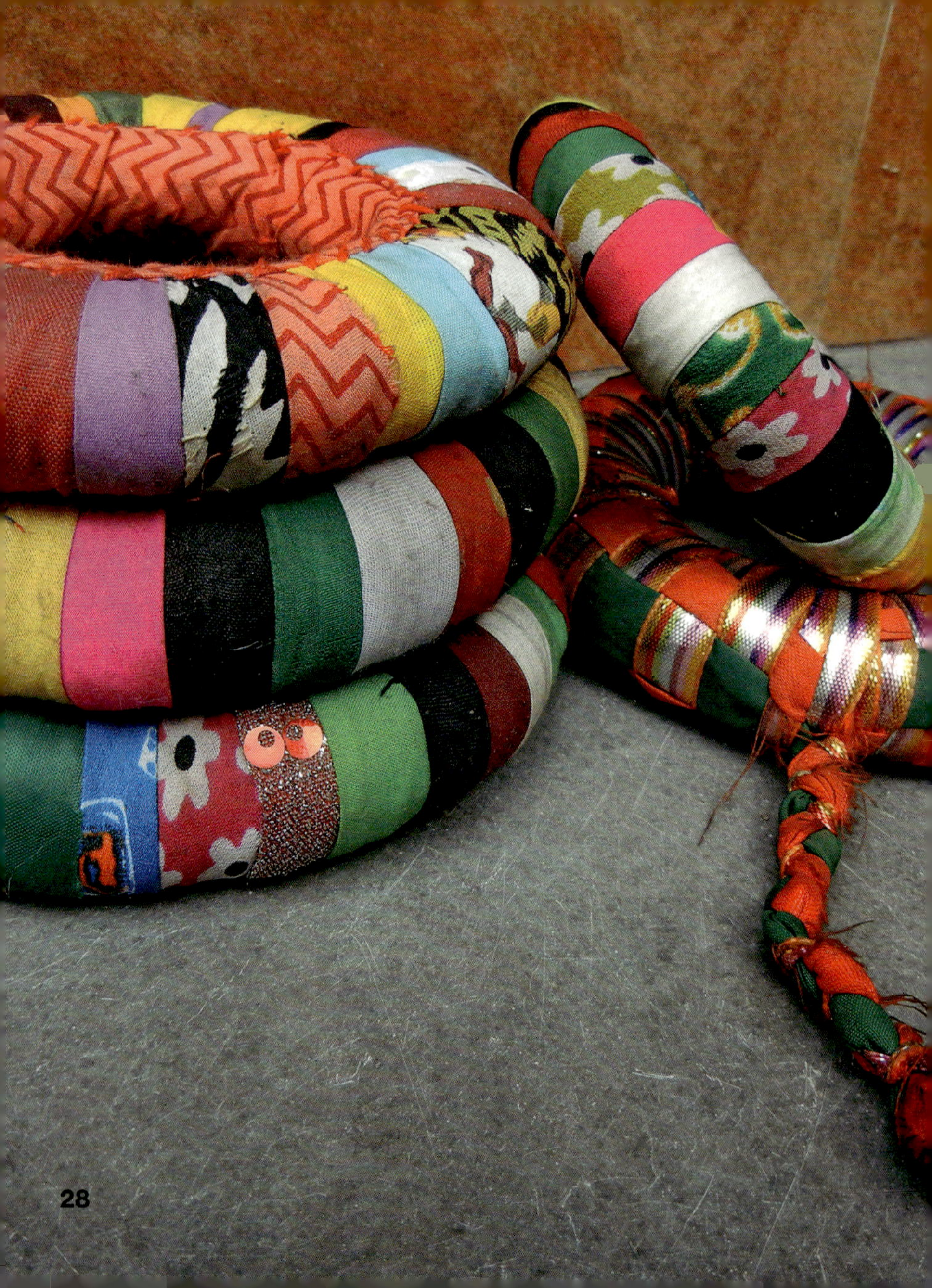

In a culture of aesthetic orientation like India's, it is the arts, particularly the plastic arts, which reveals the culture's organic development and patterns of continuity more clearly and more tangibly than any other cultural activity.

~ Richard Lannoy
The Speaking Tree

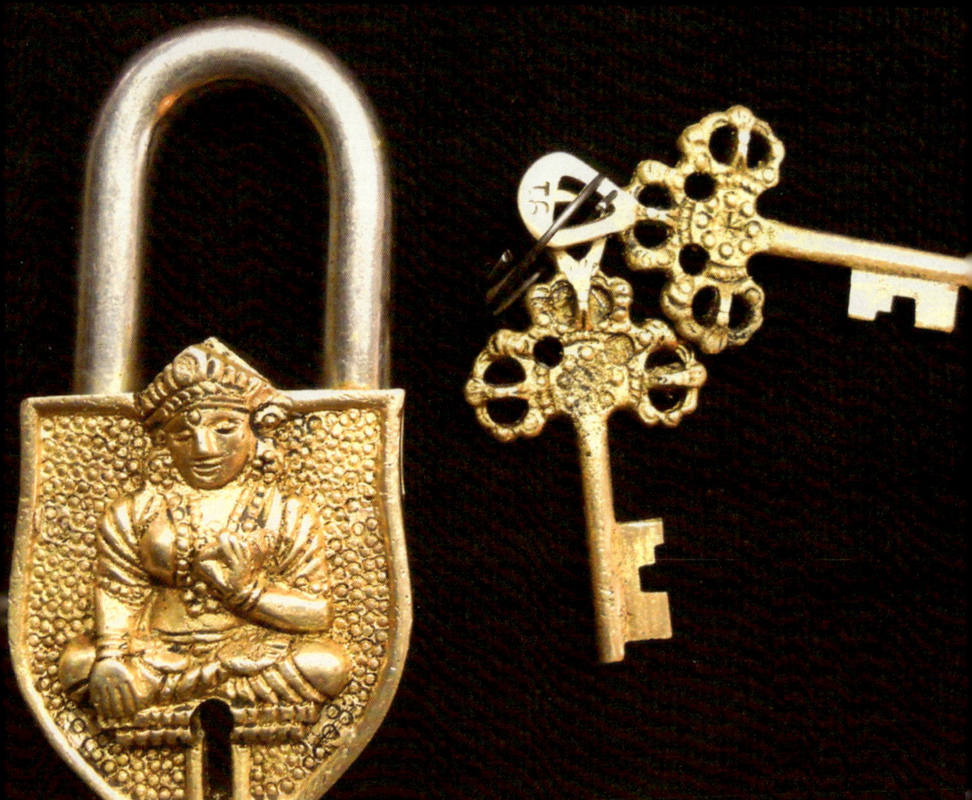

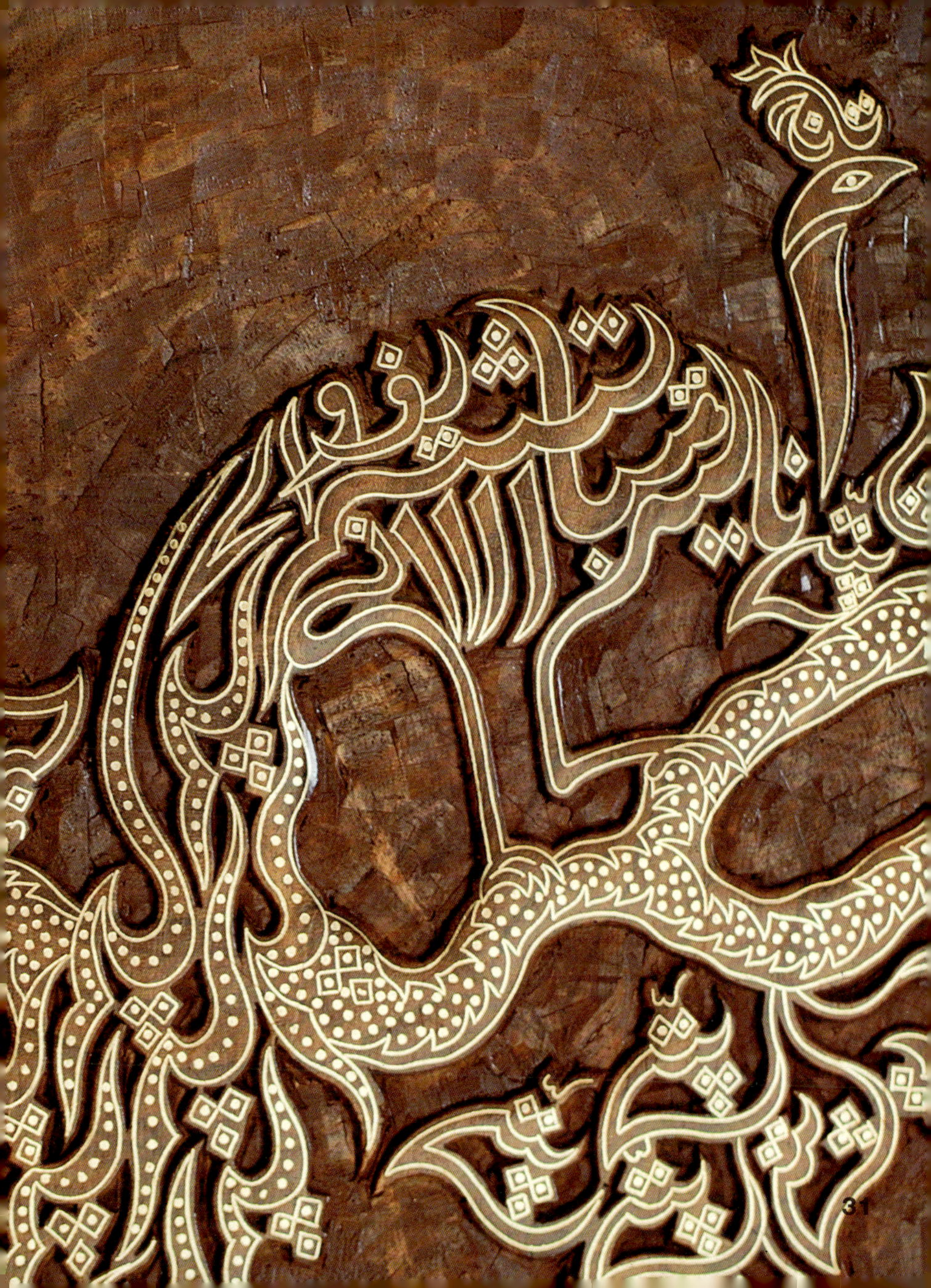

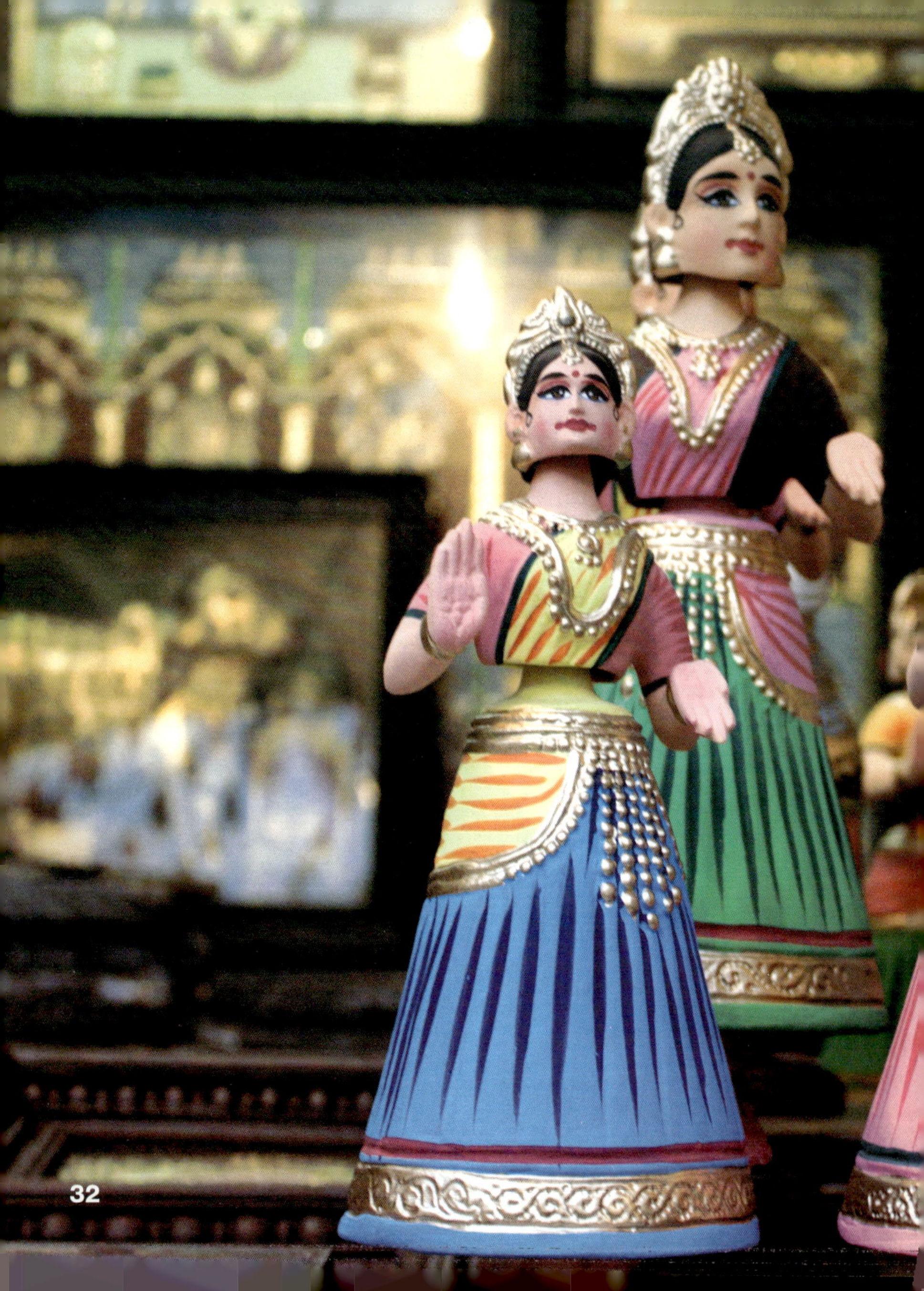

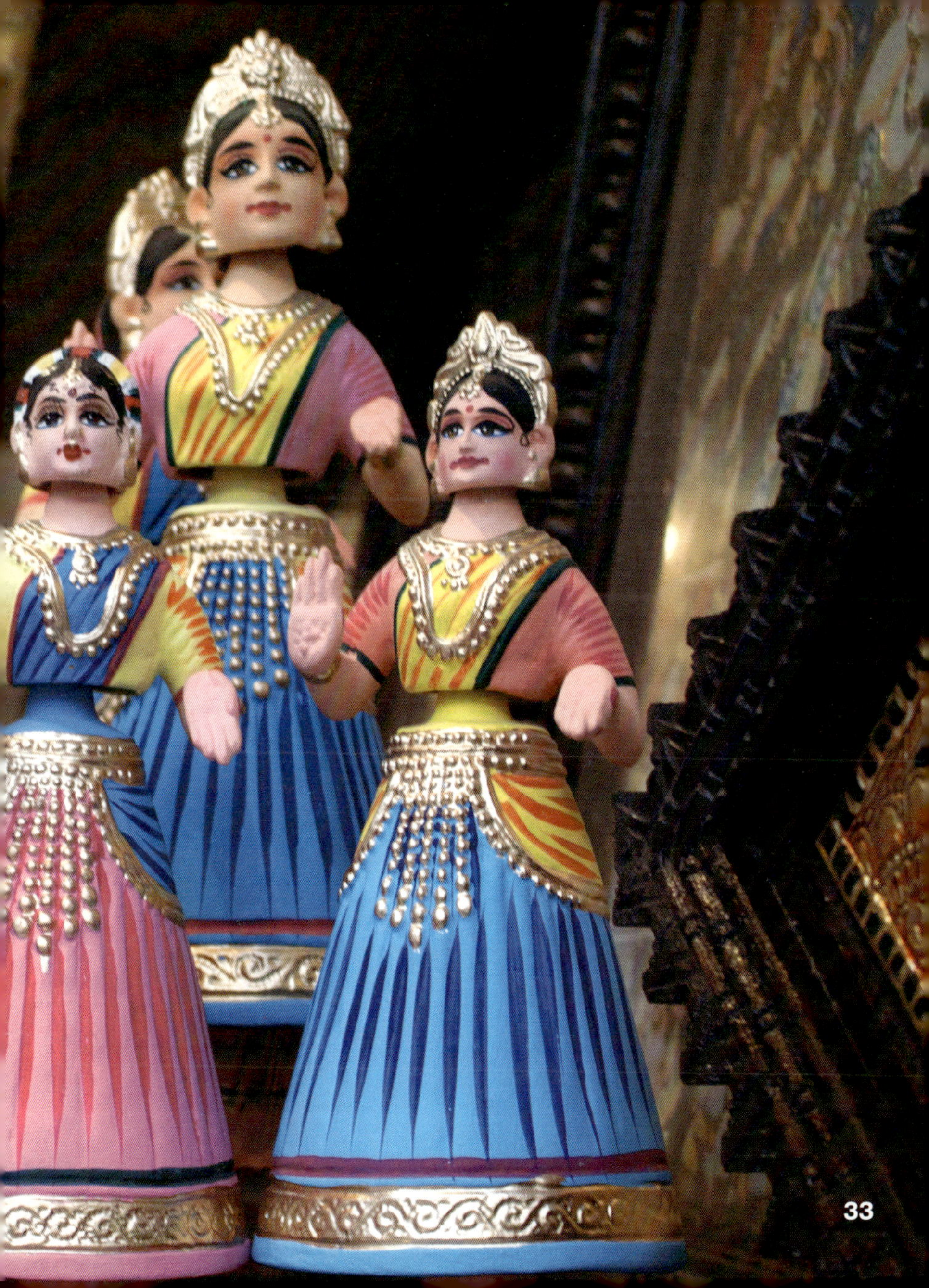

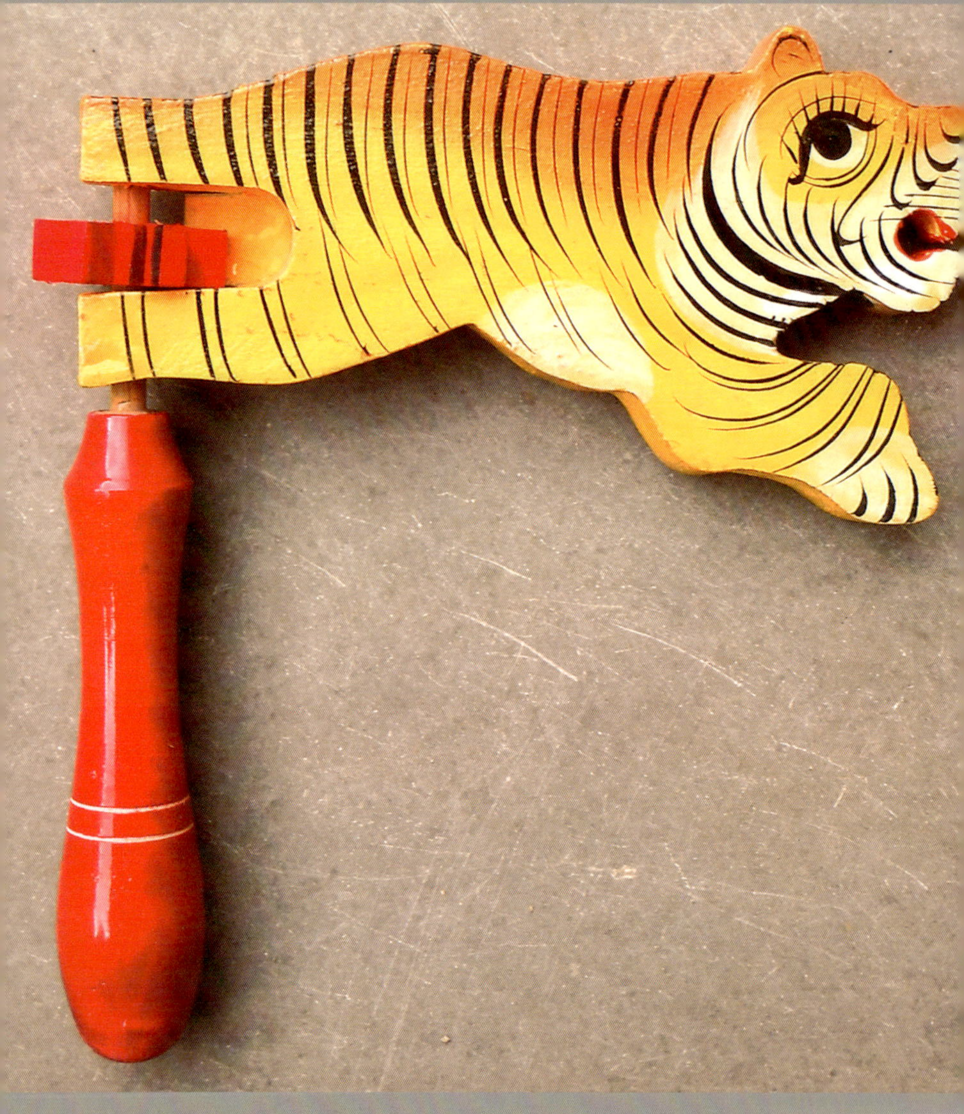

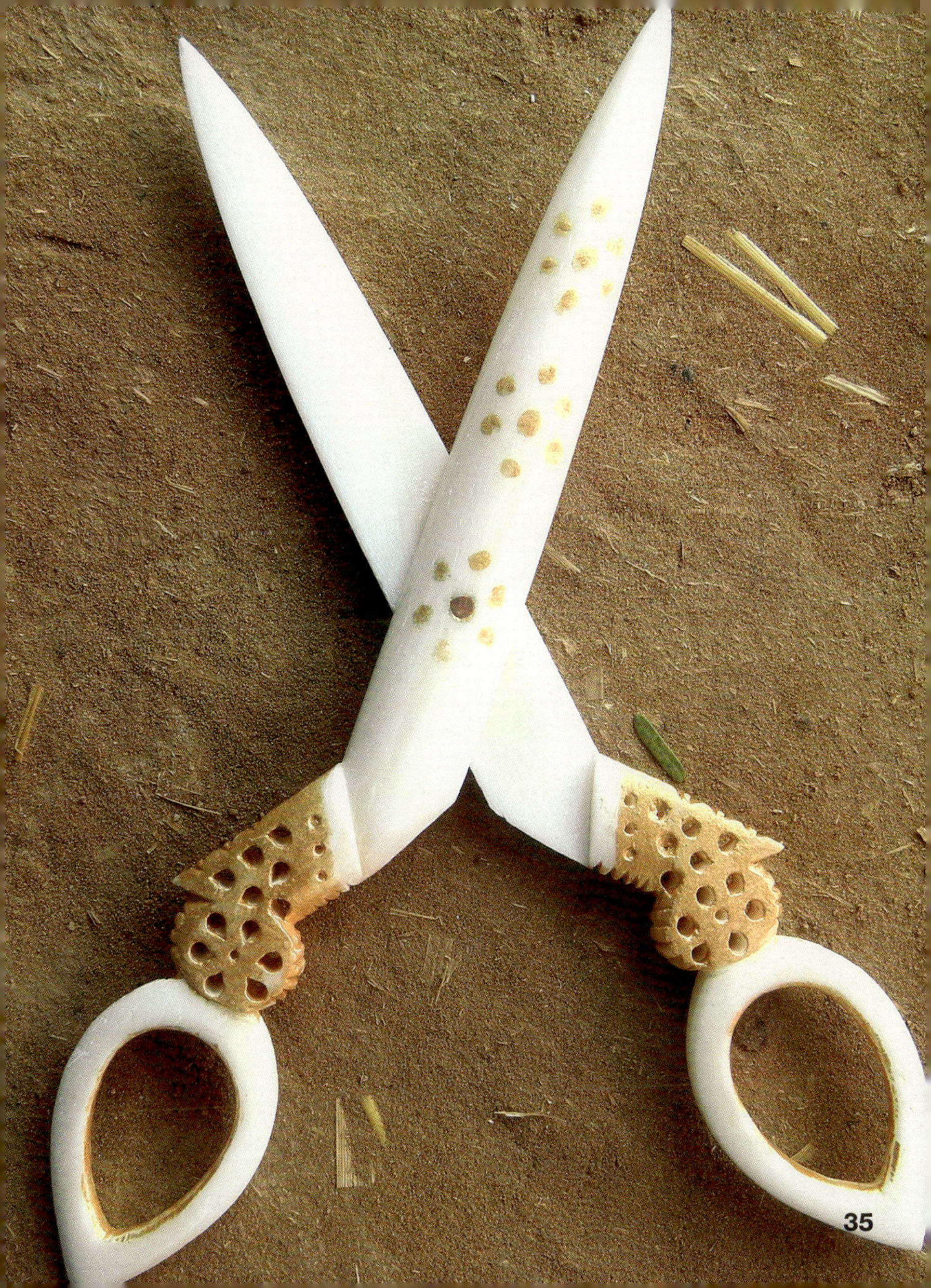

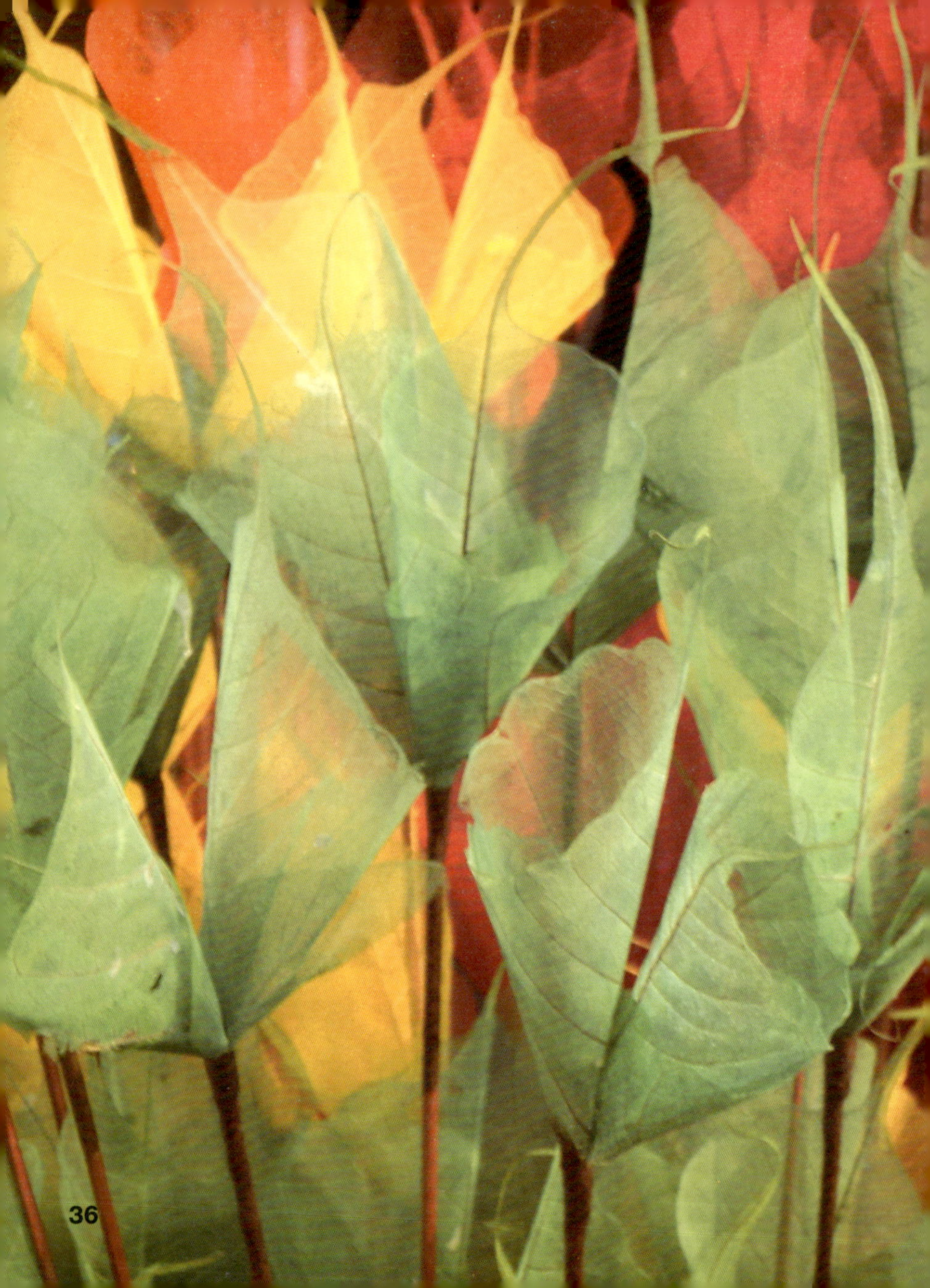

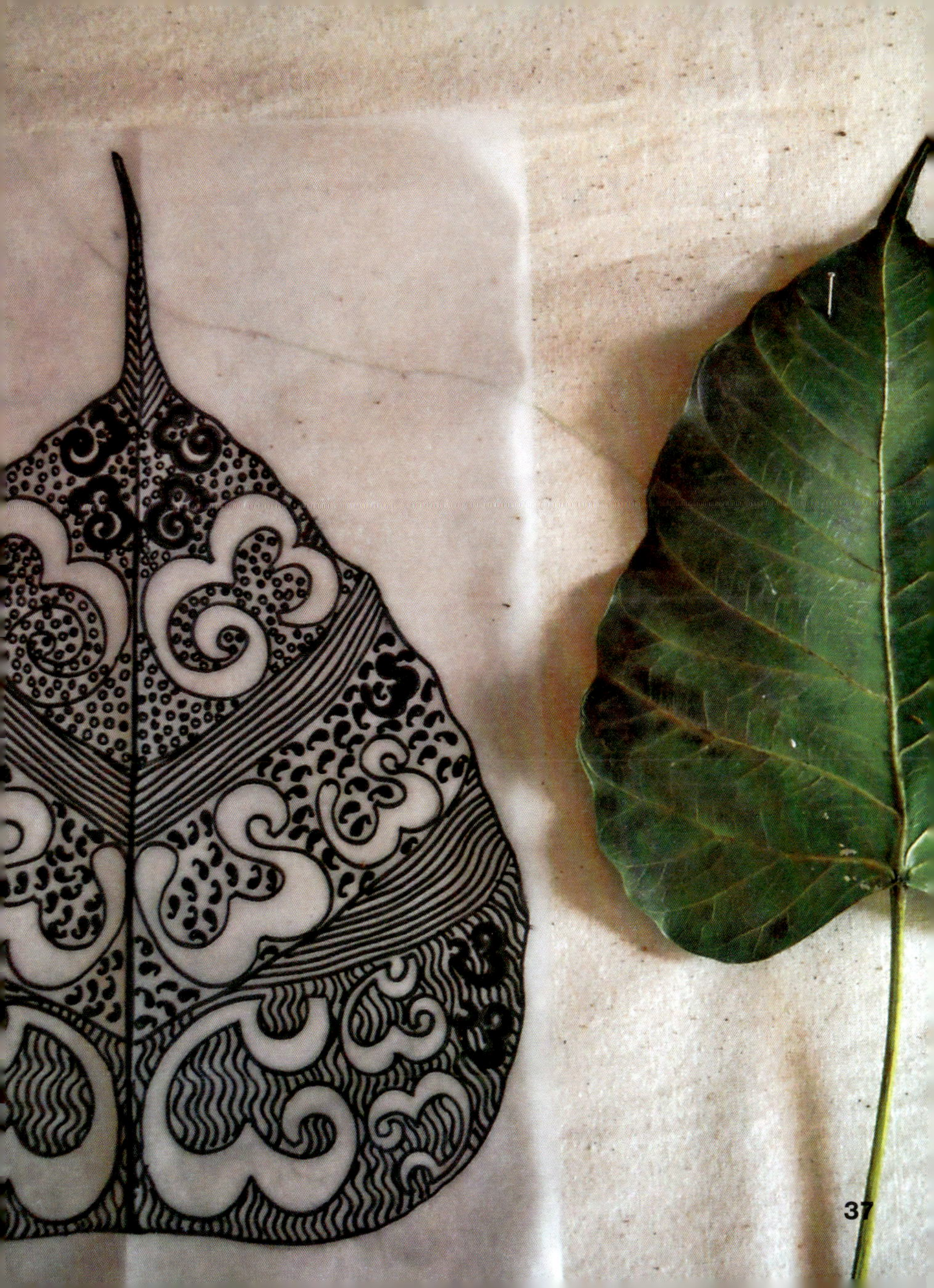

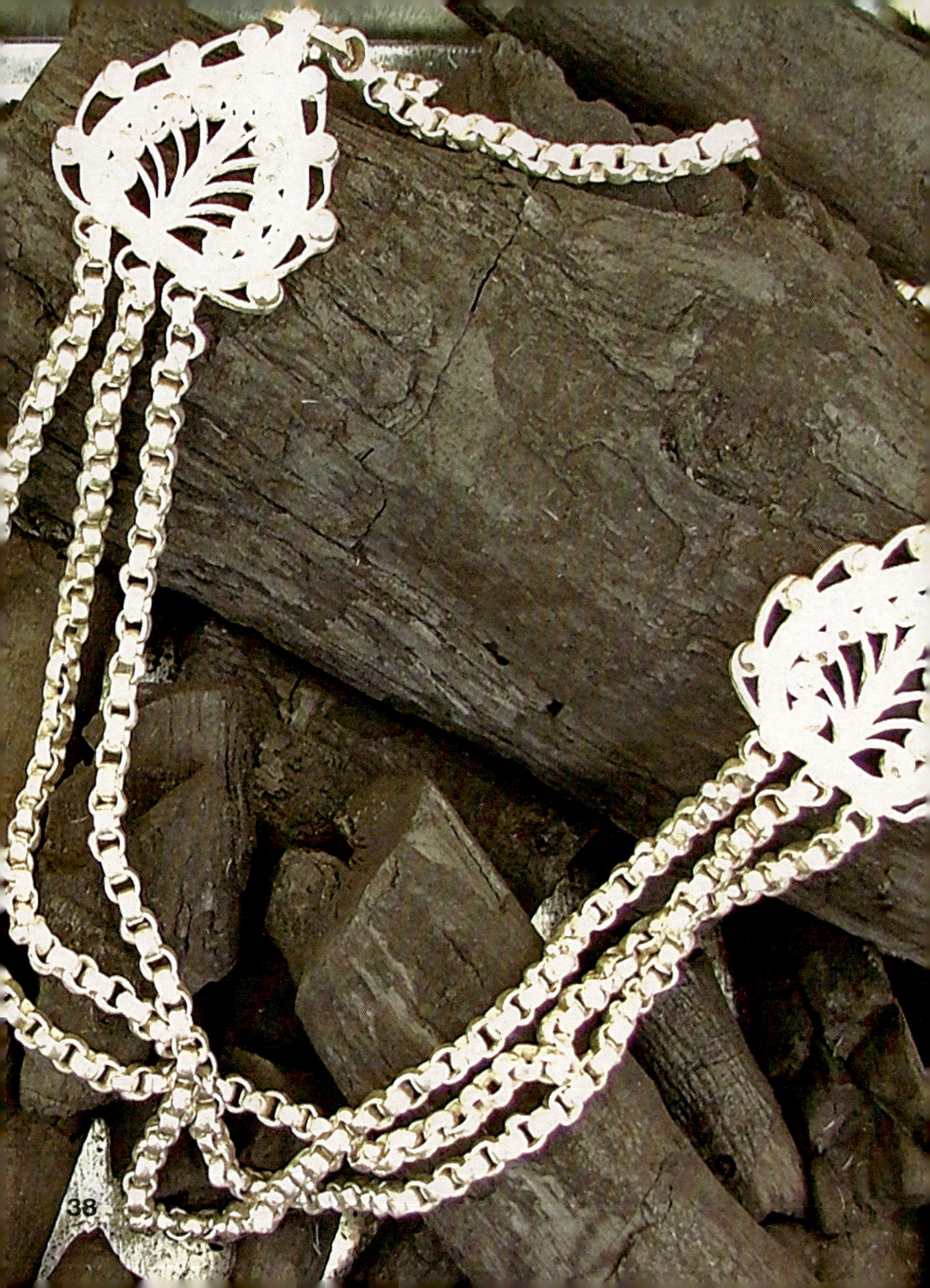

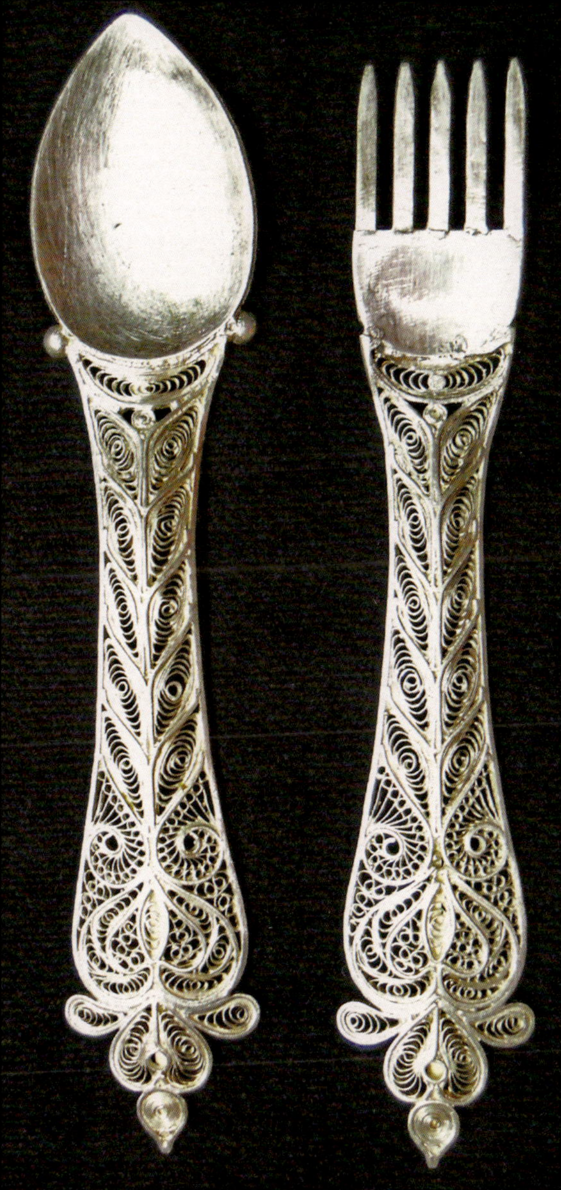

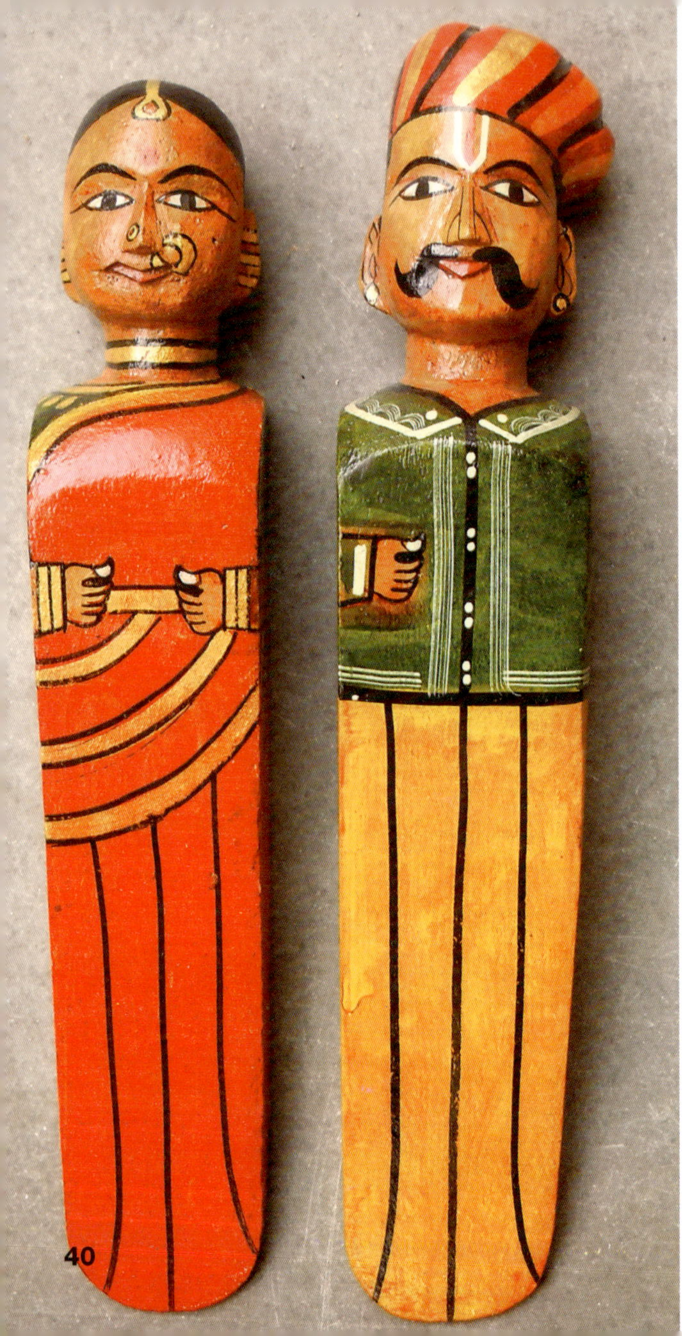

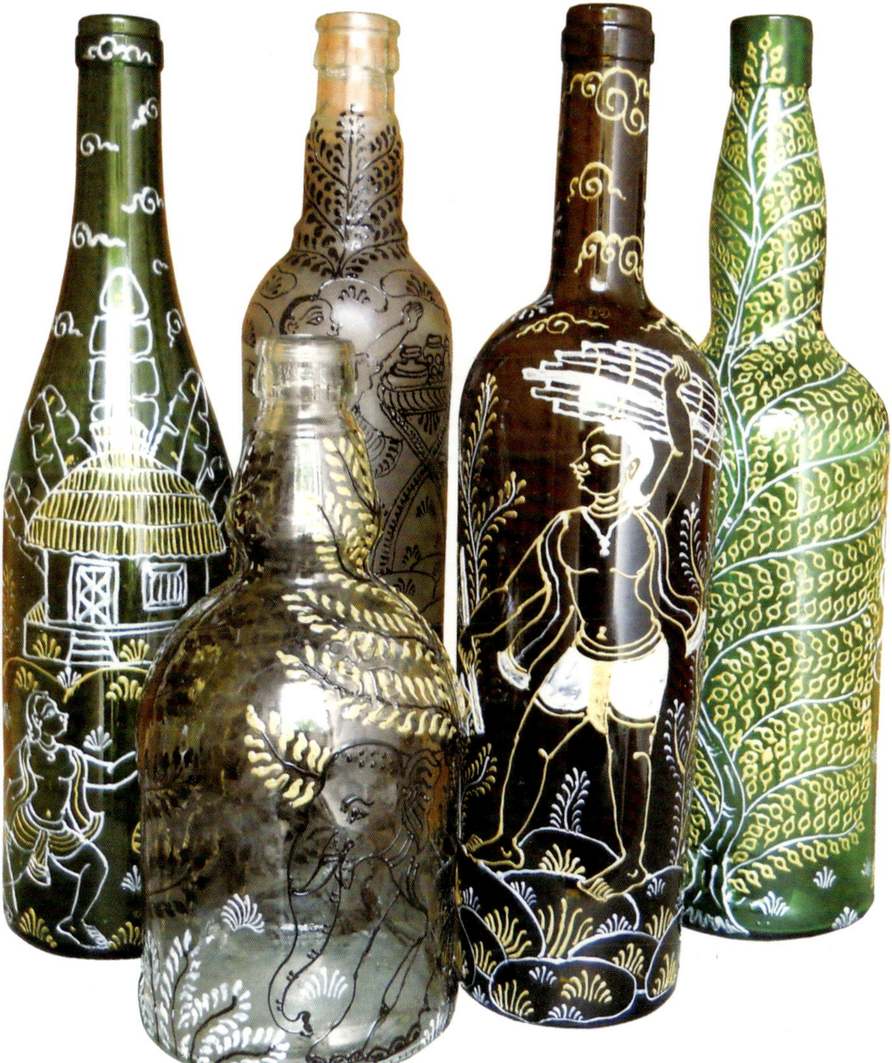

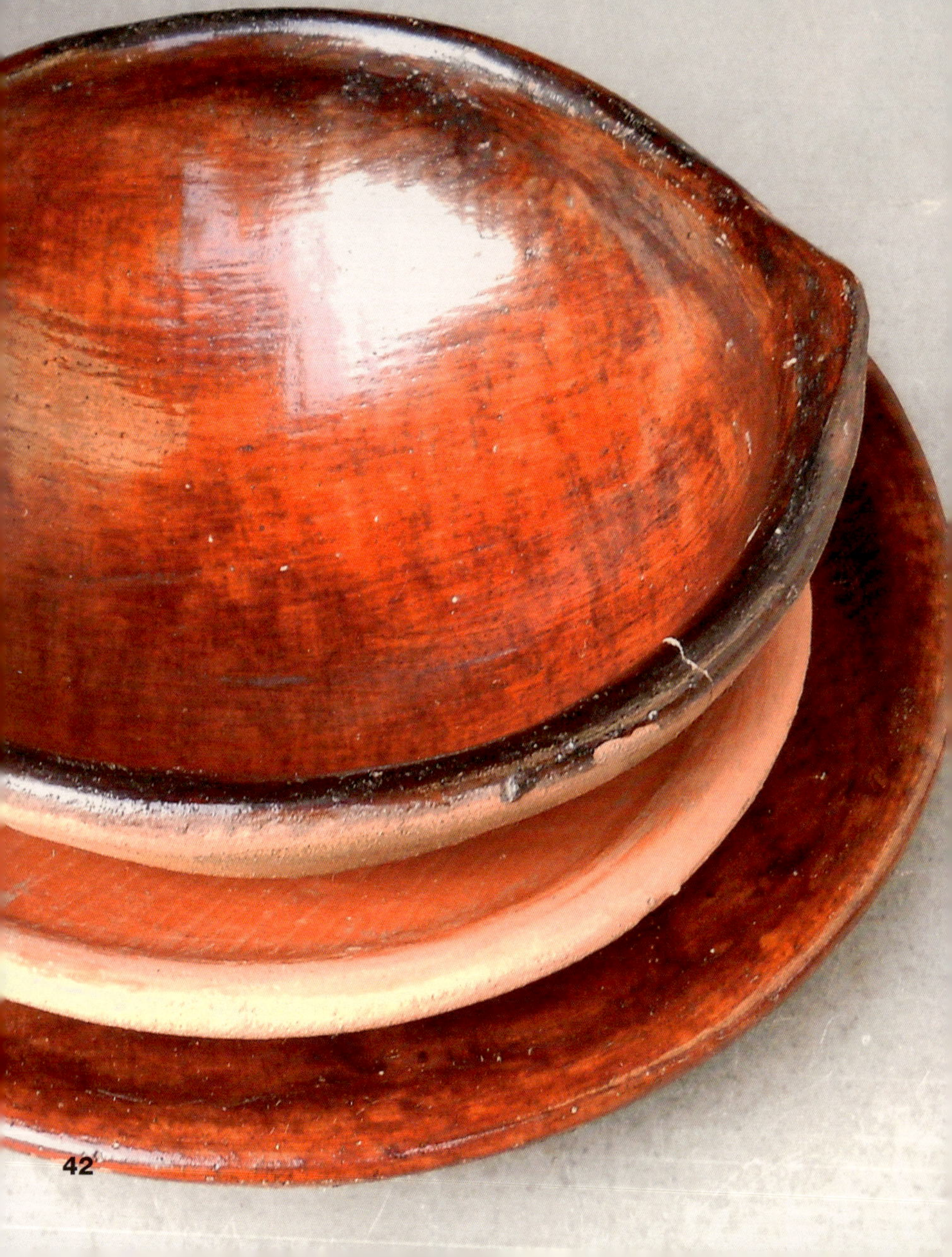

Once more a view of the bazaar as particular kinds of relationships among persons is brought home to us. In this scheme the idea of the person is culturally constructed and relationships are culturally differentiated. The links among persons in the bazaar are forged in many directions on many levels. At the same time the understanding of persons in their bazaar relationships cannot be confused with other kinds of relationships.

~ Ákos Óstór
Culture and Power

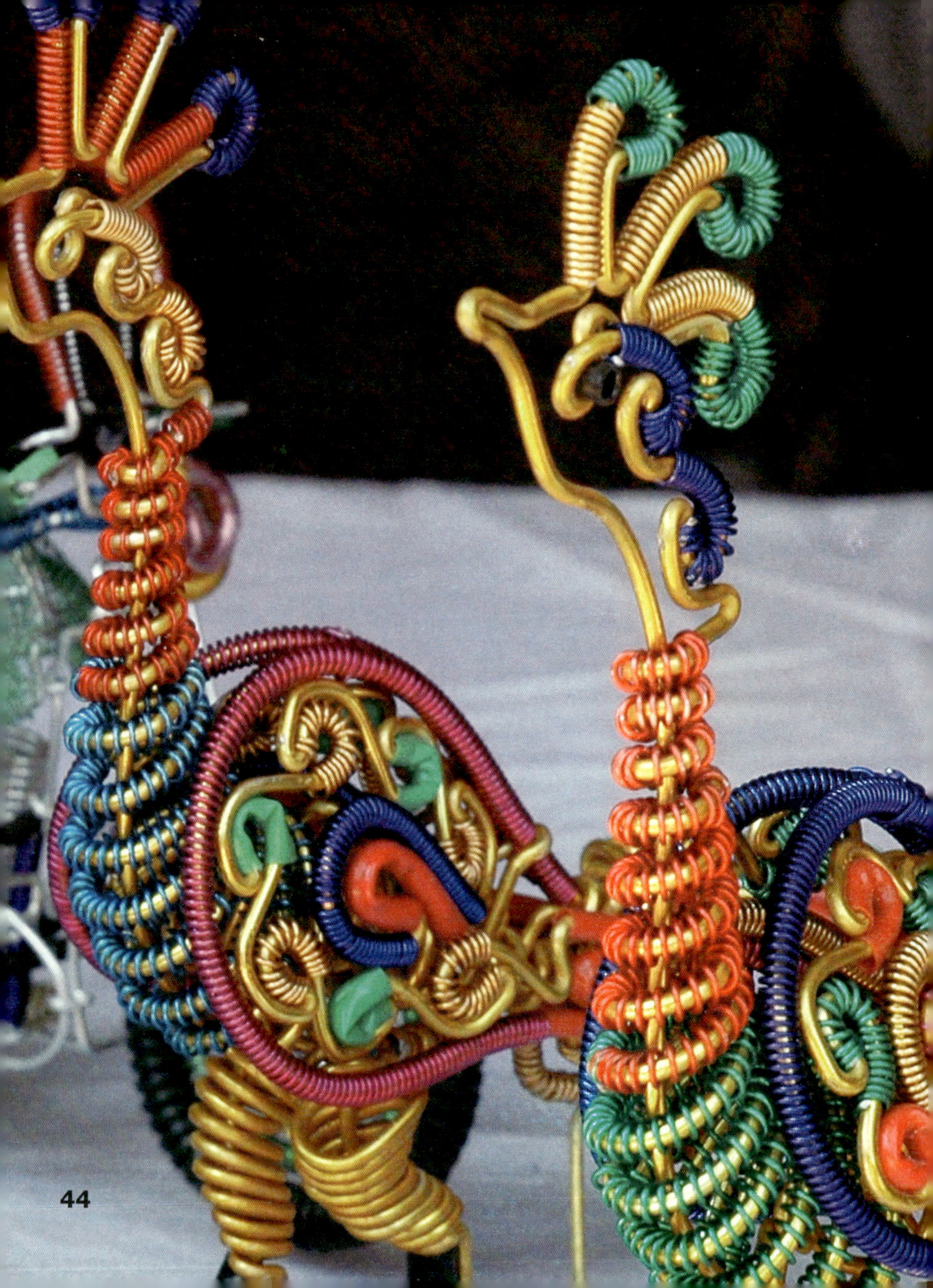

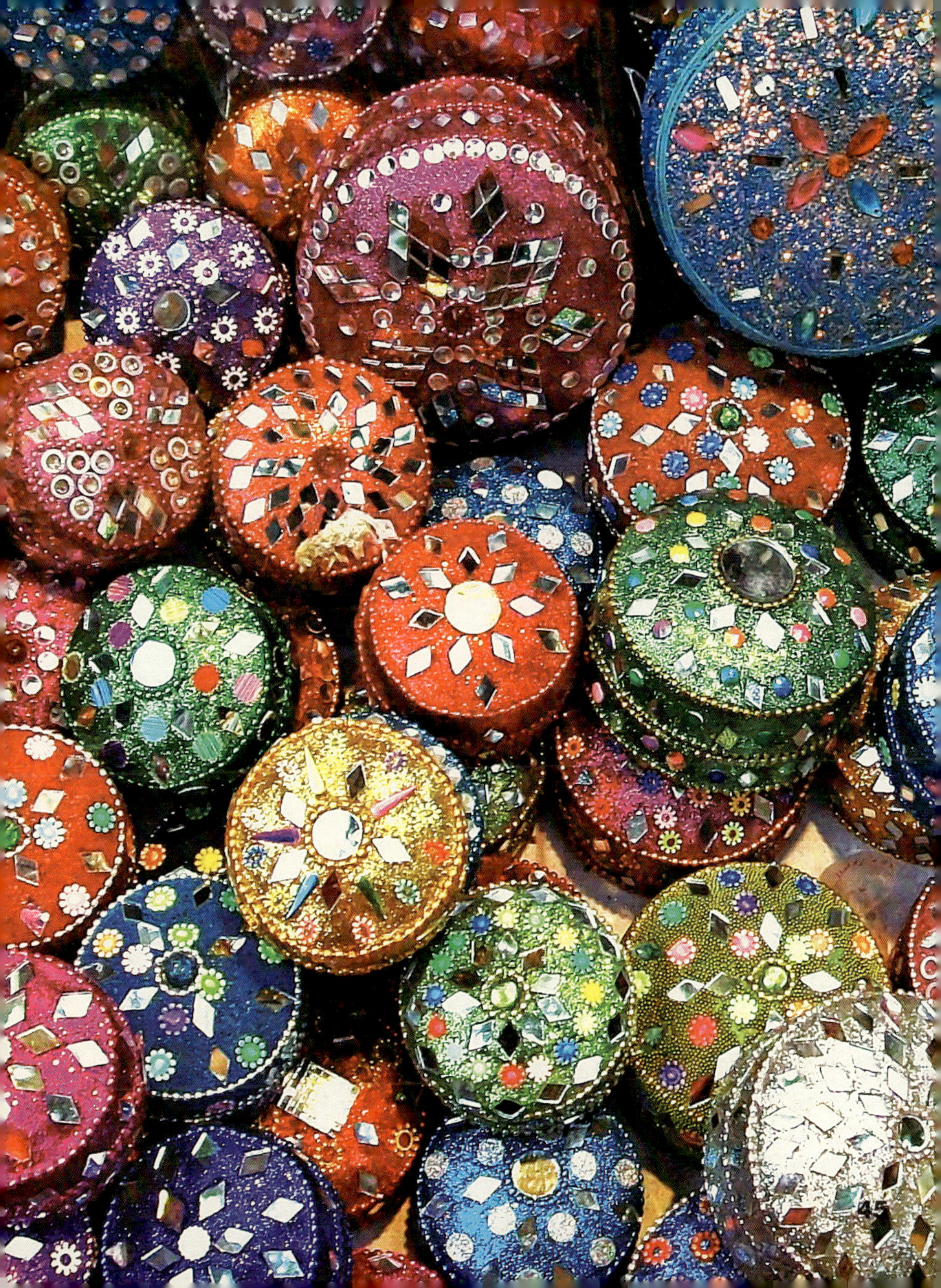

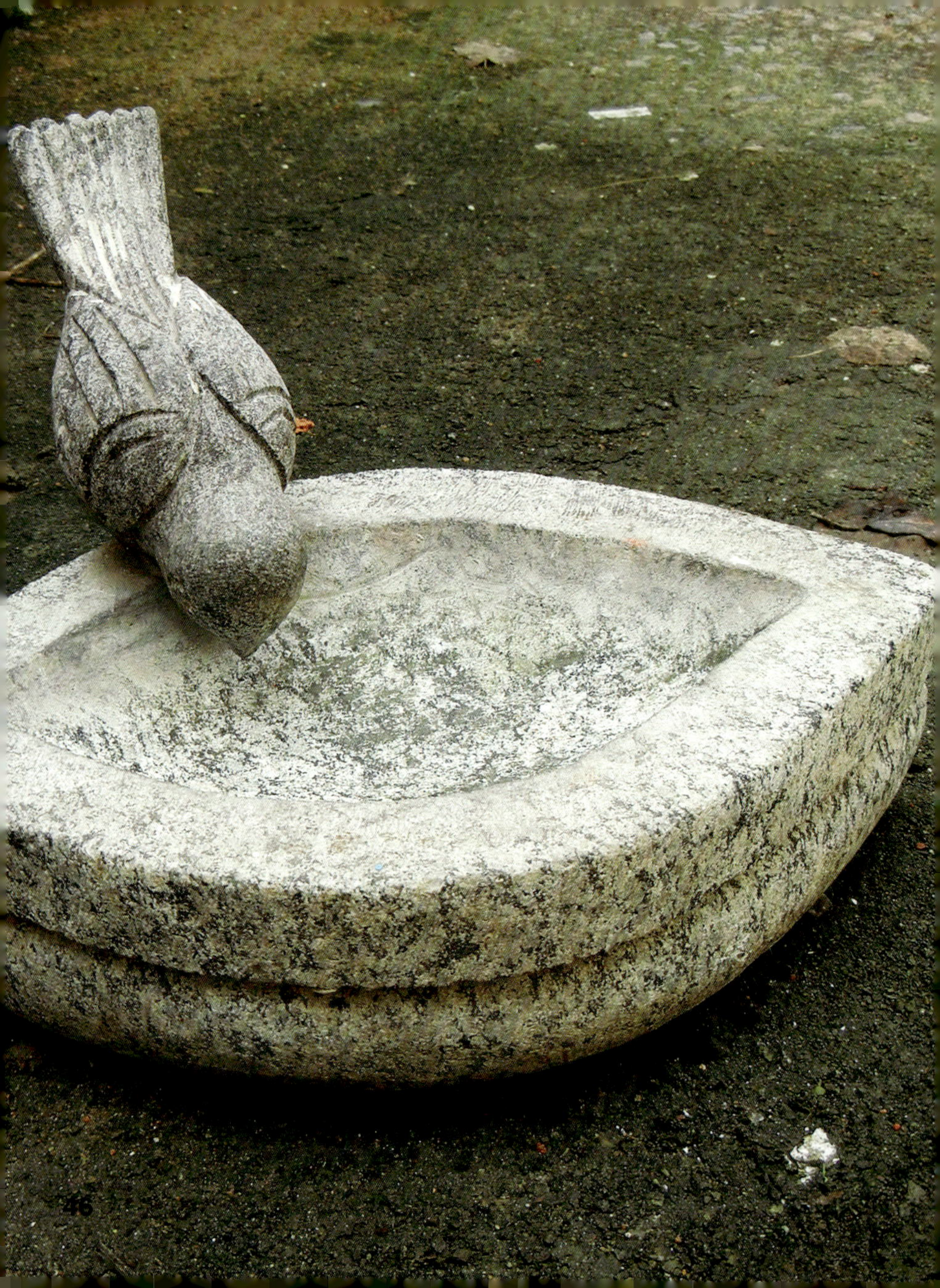

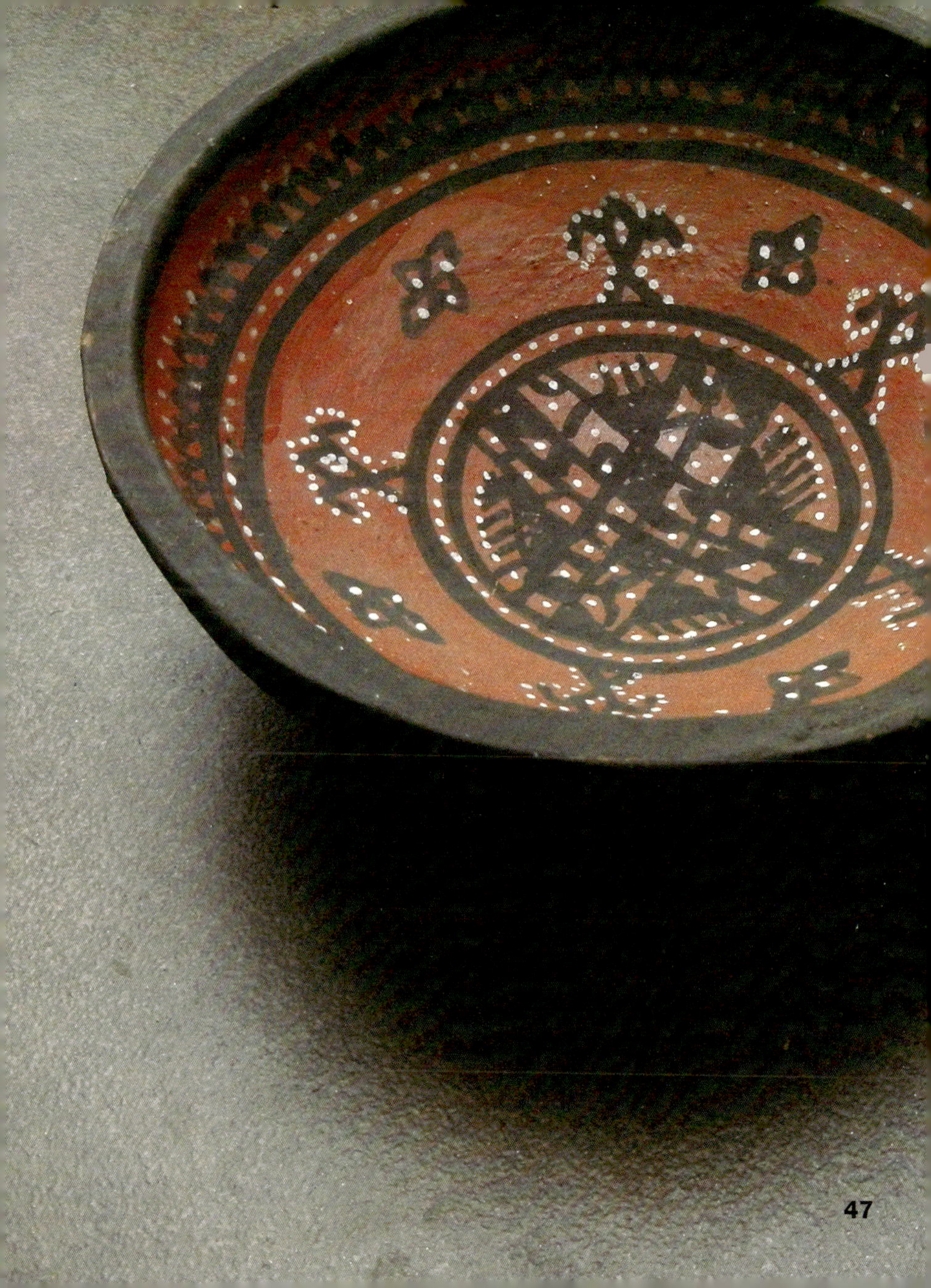

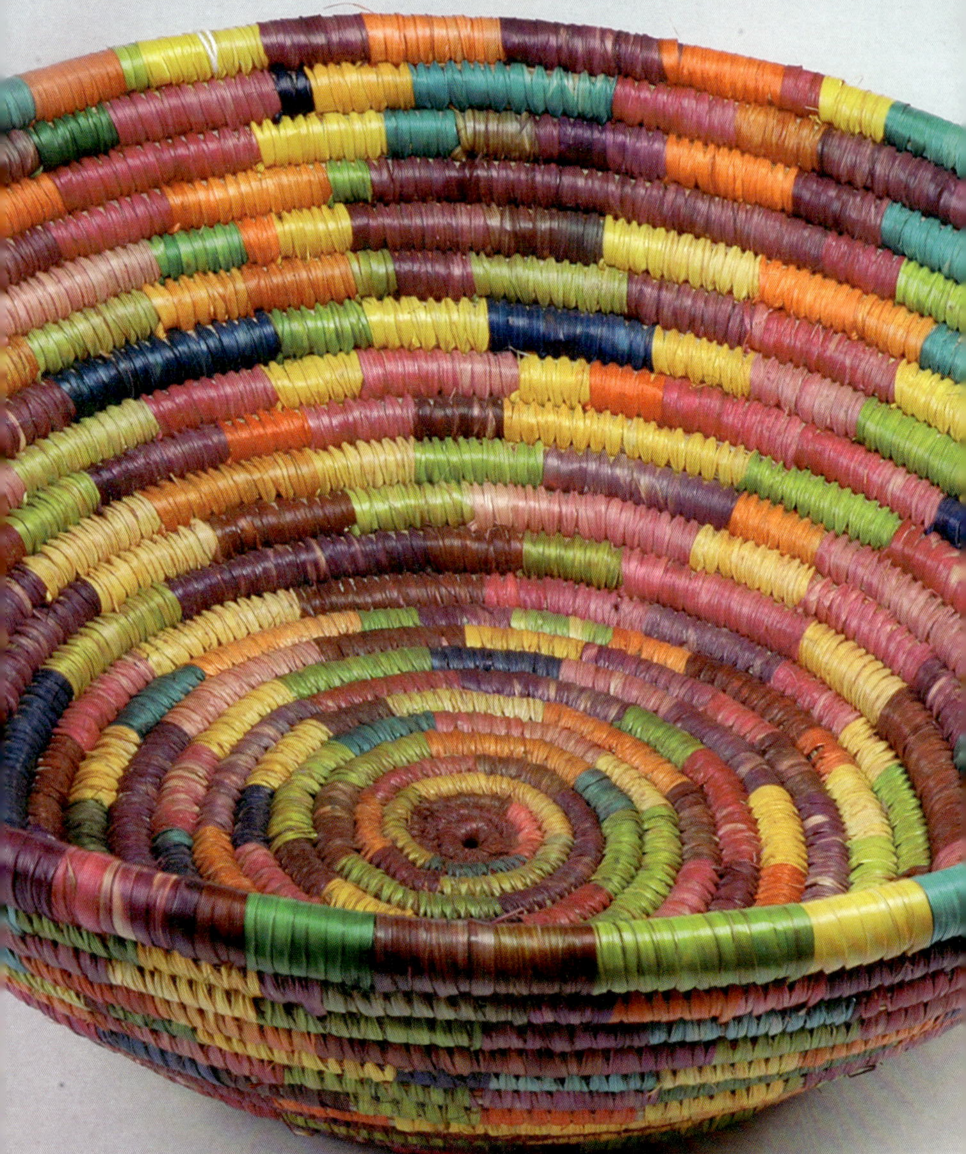

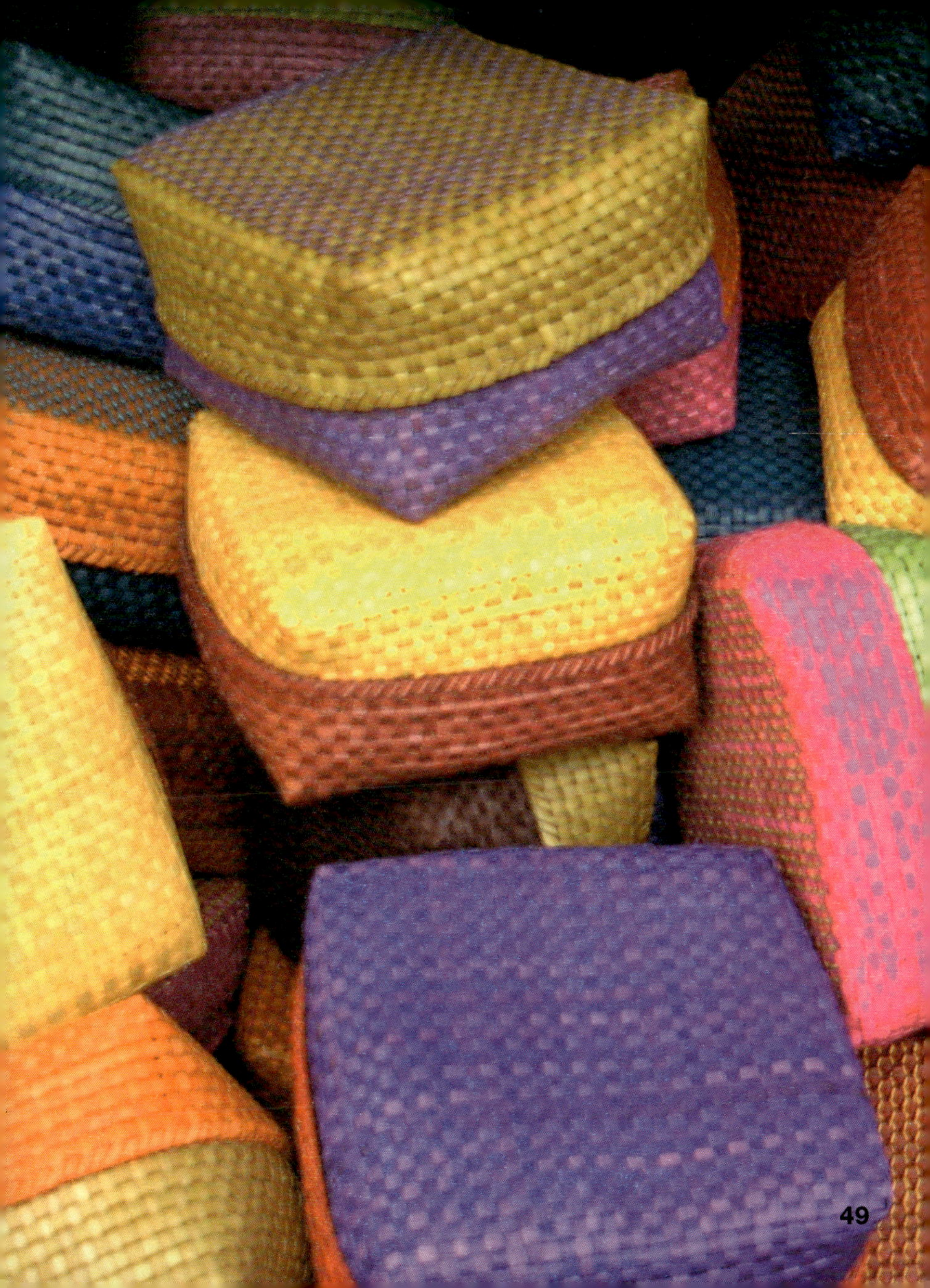

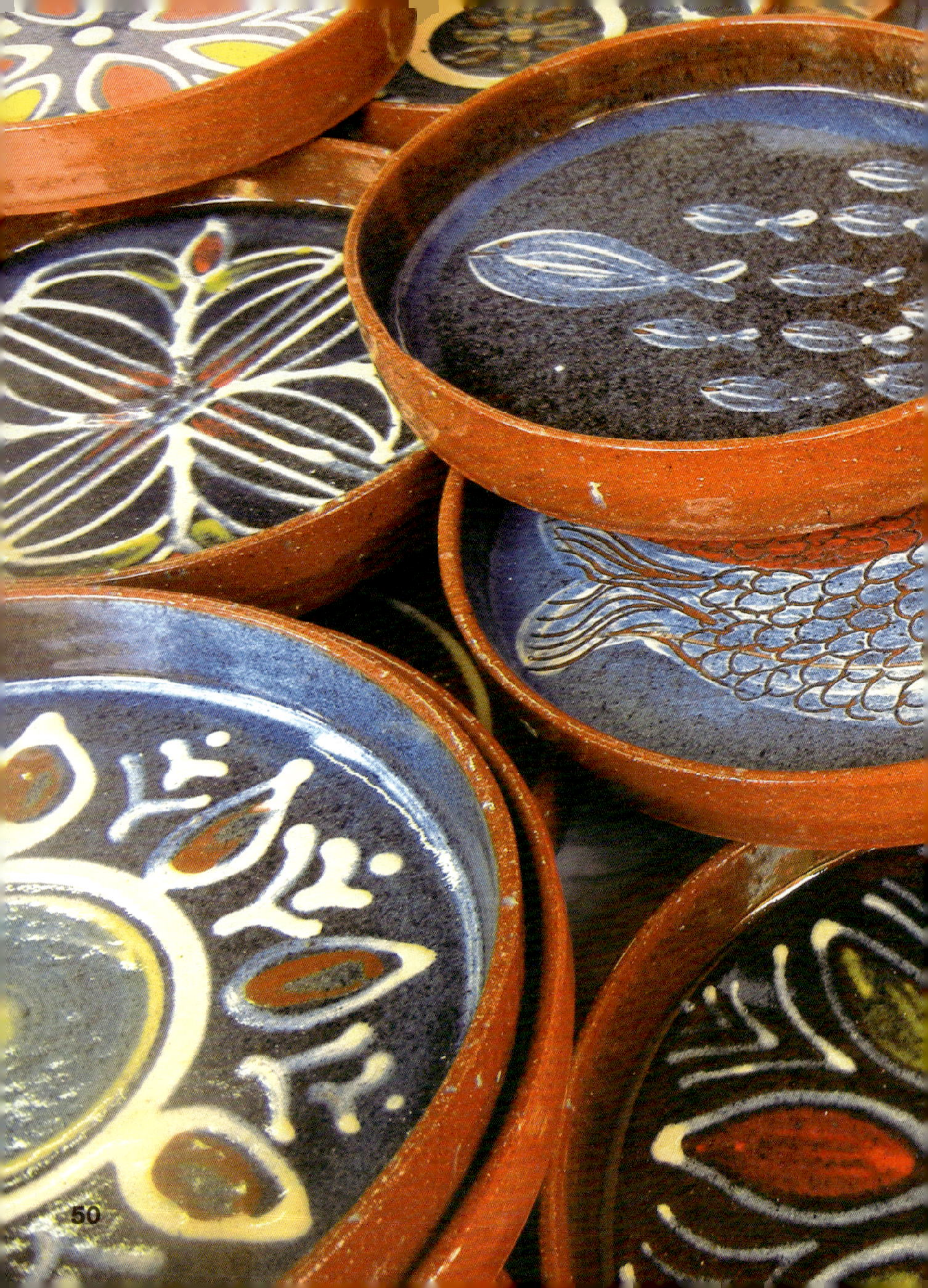

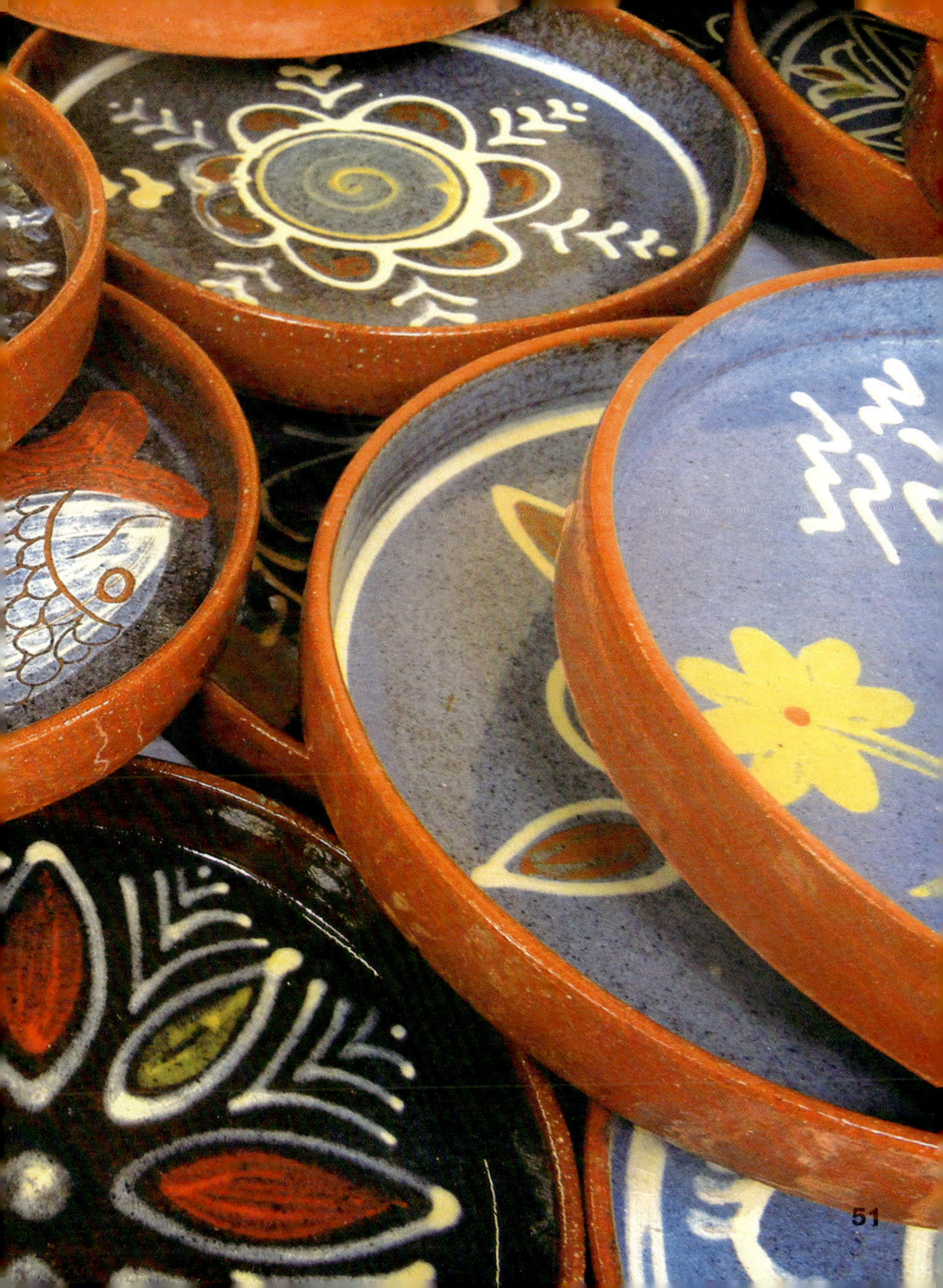

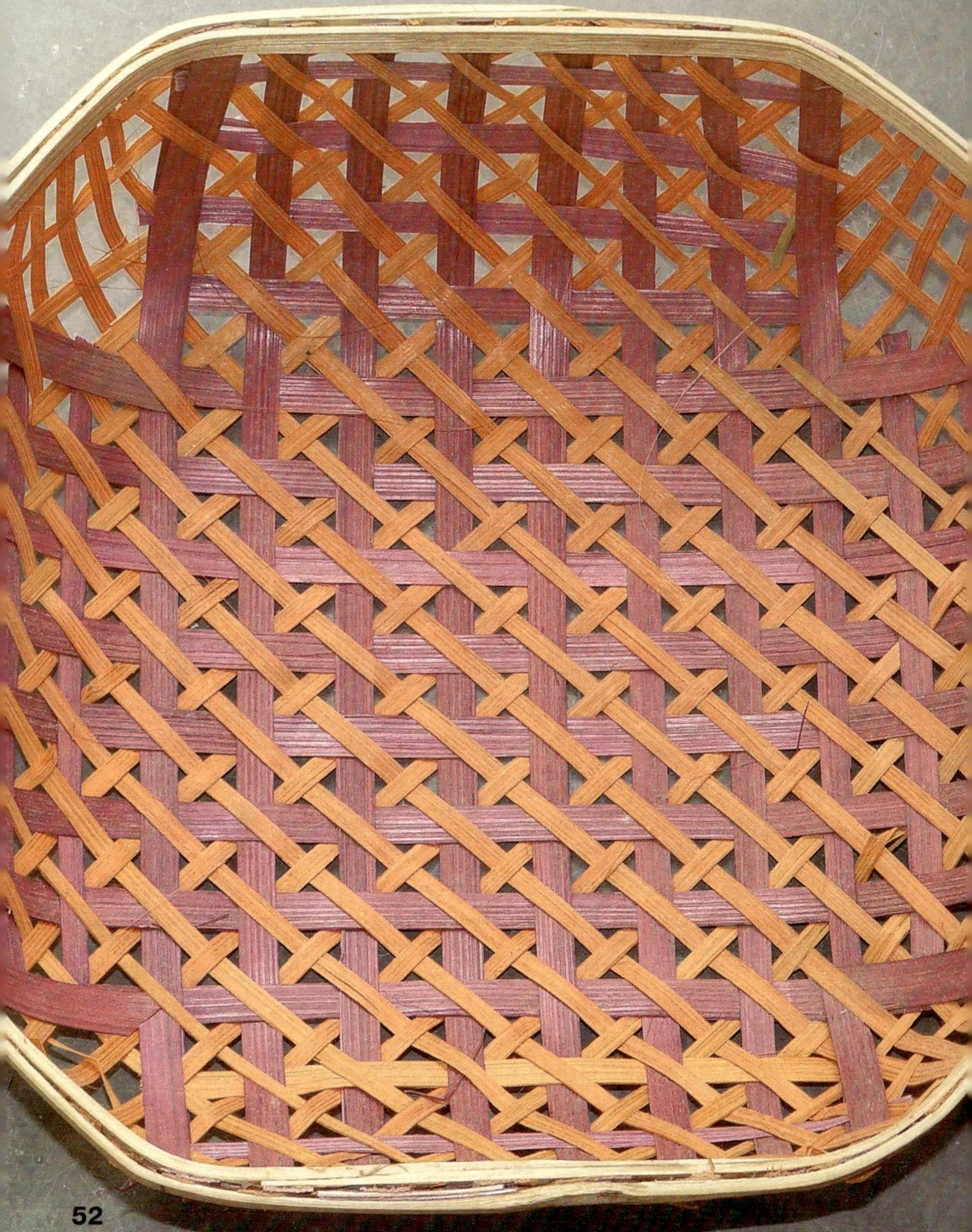

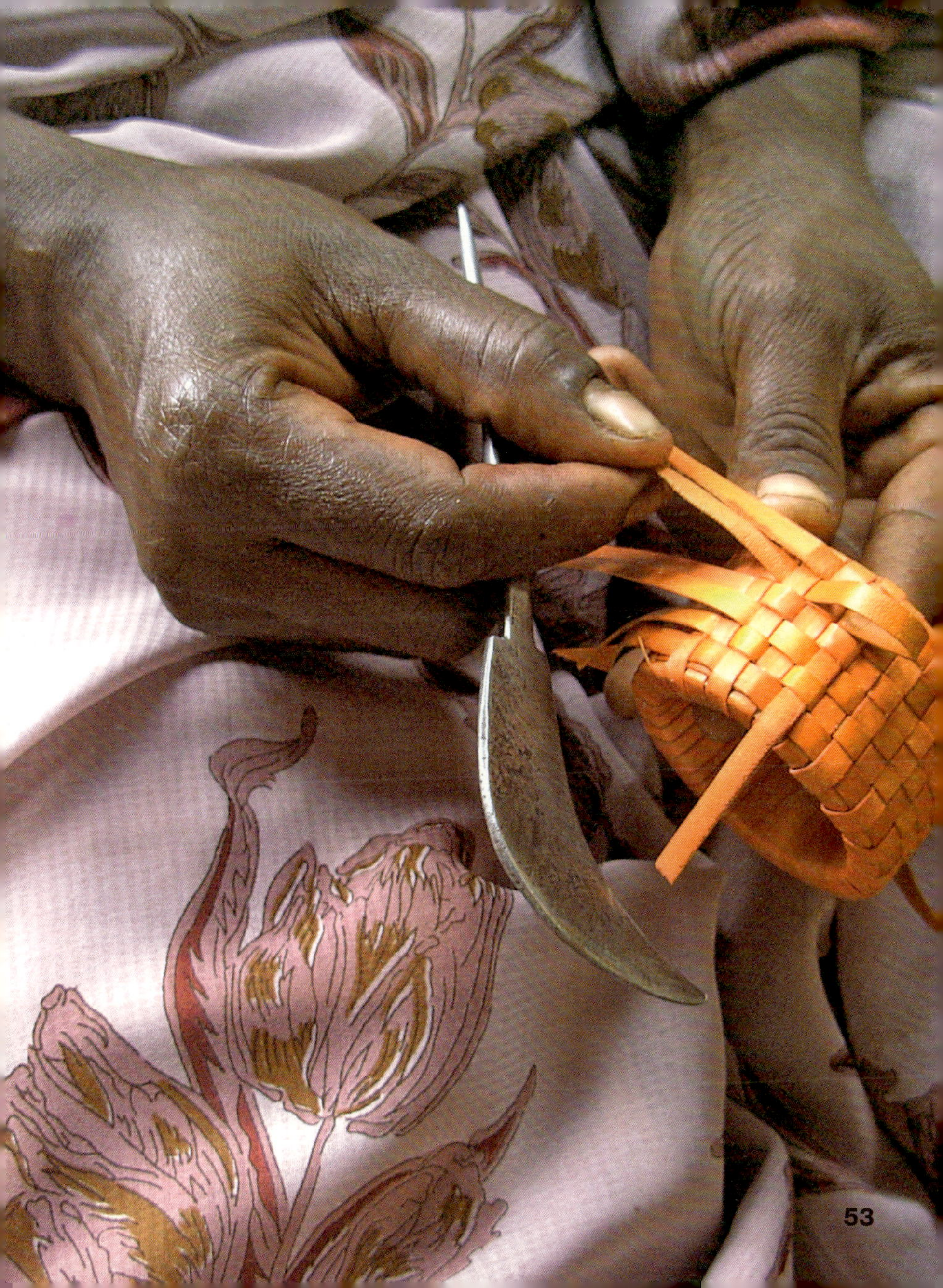

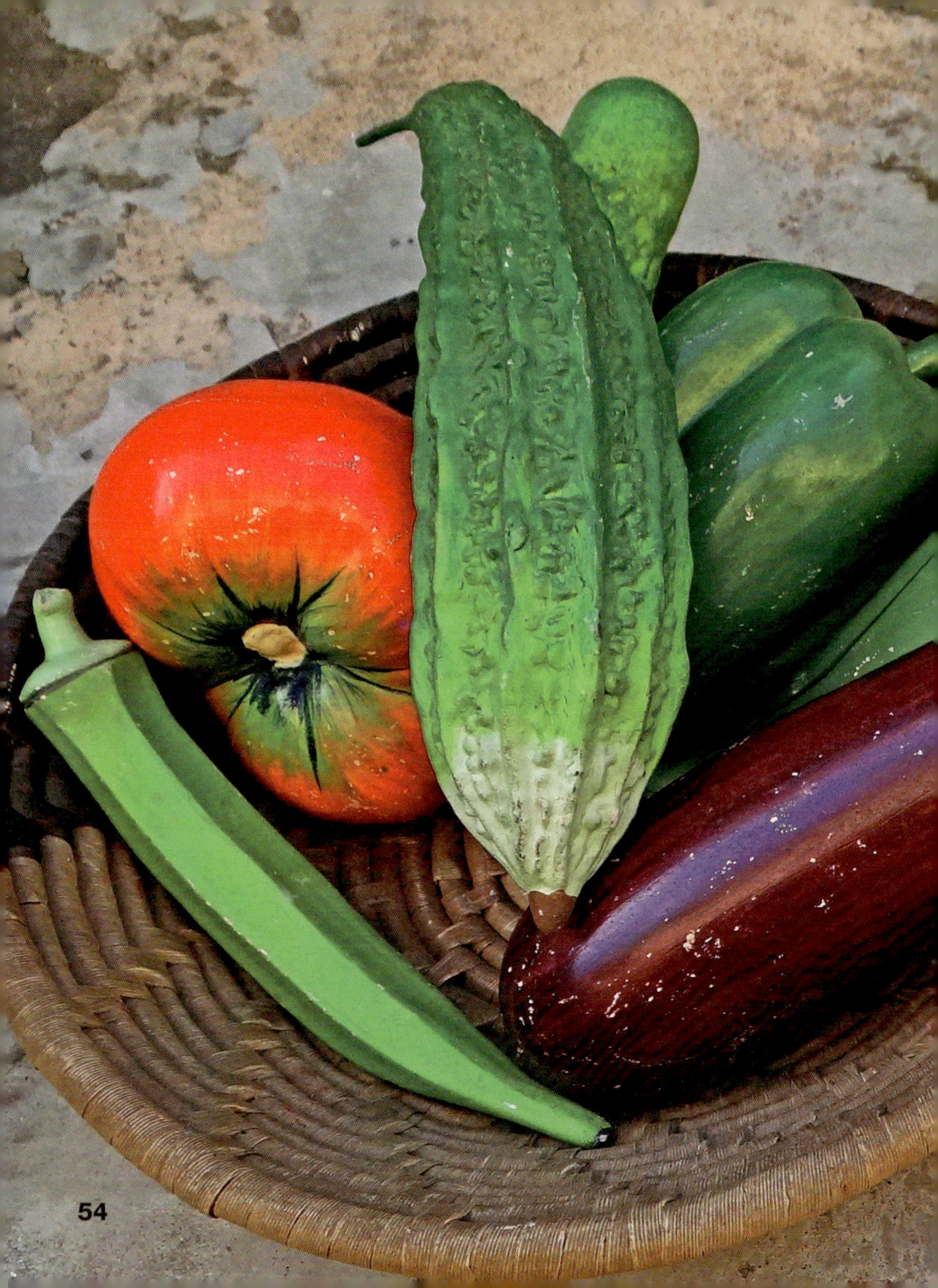

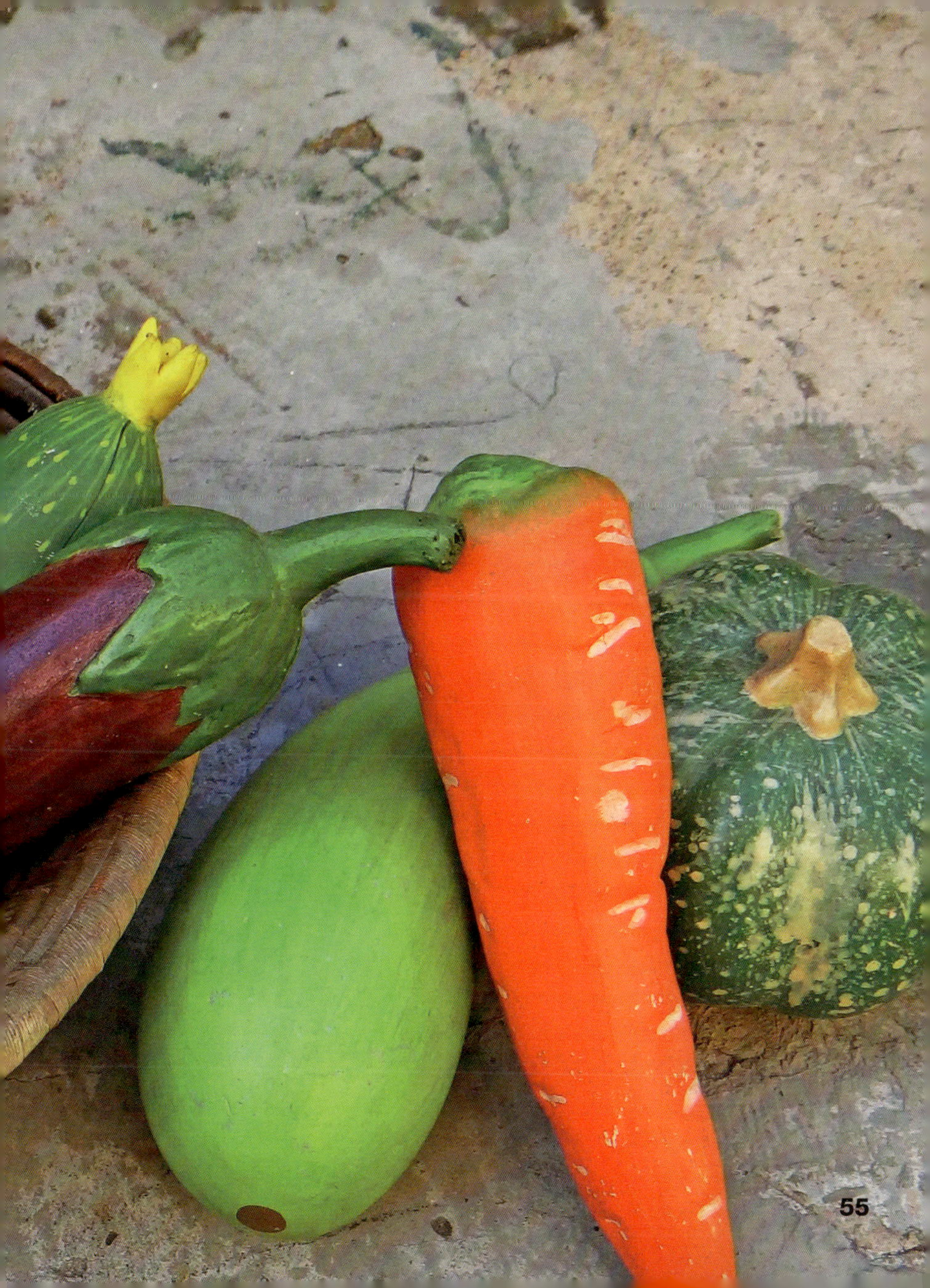

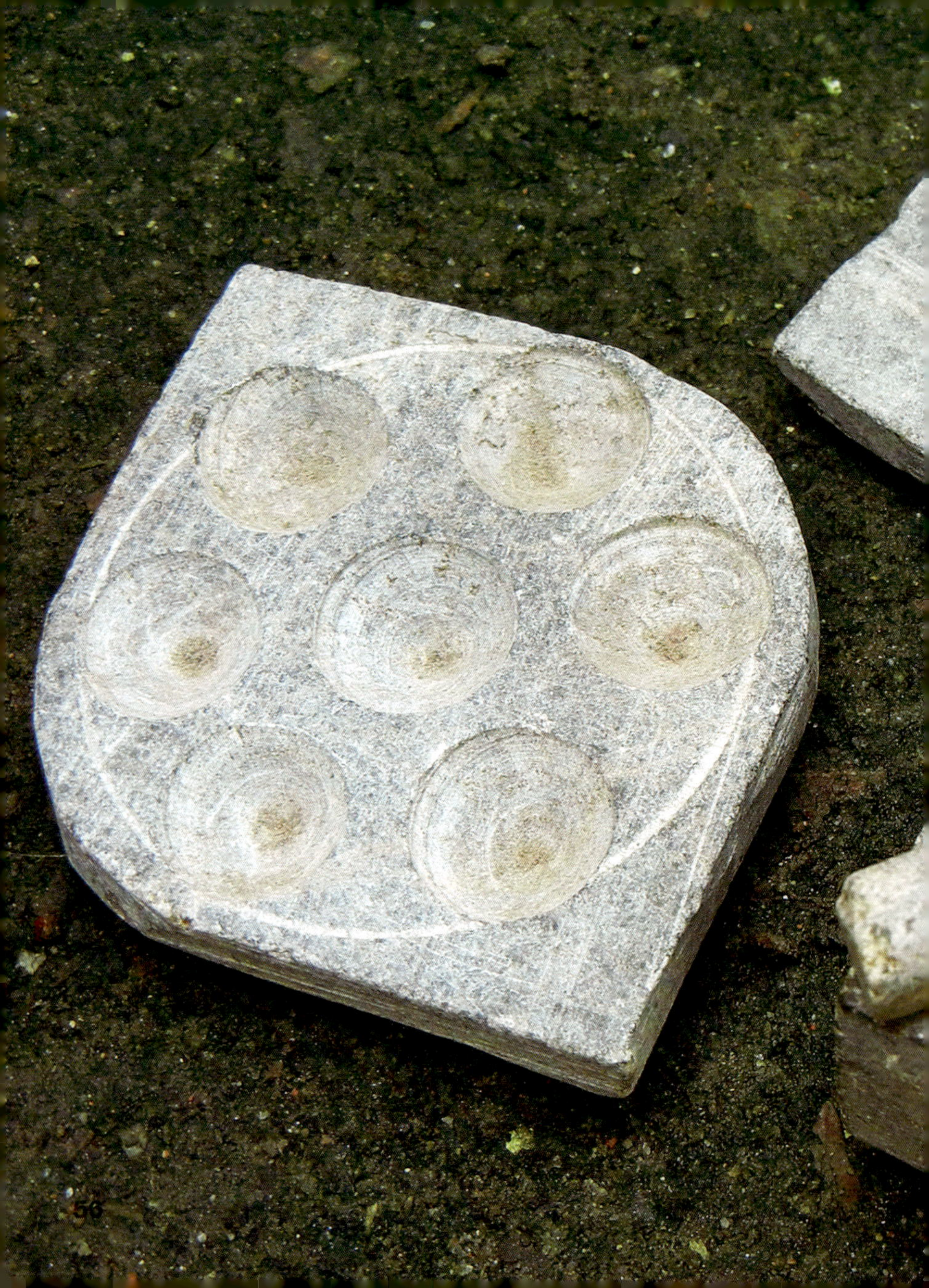

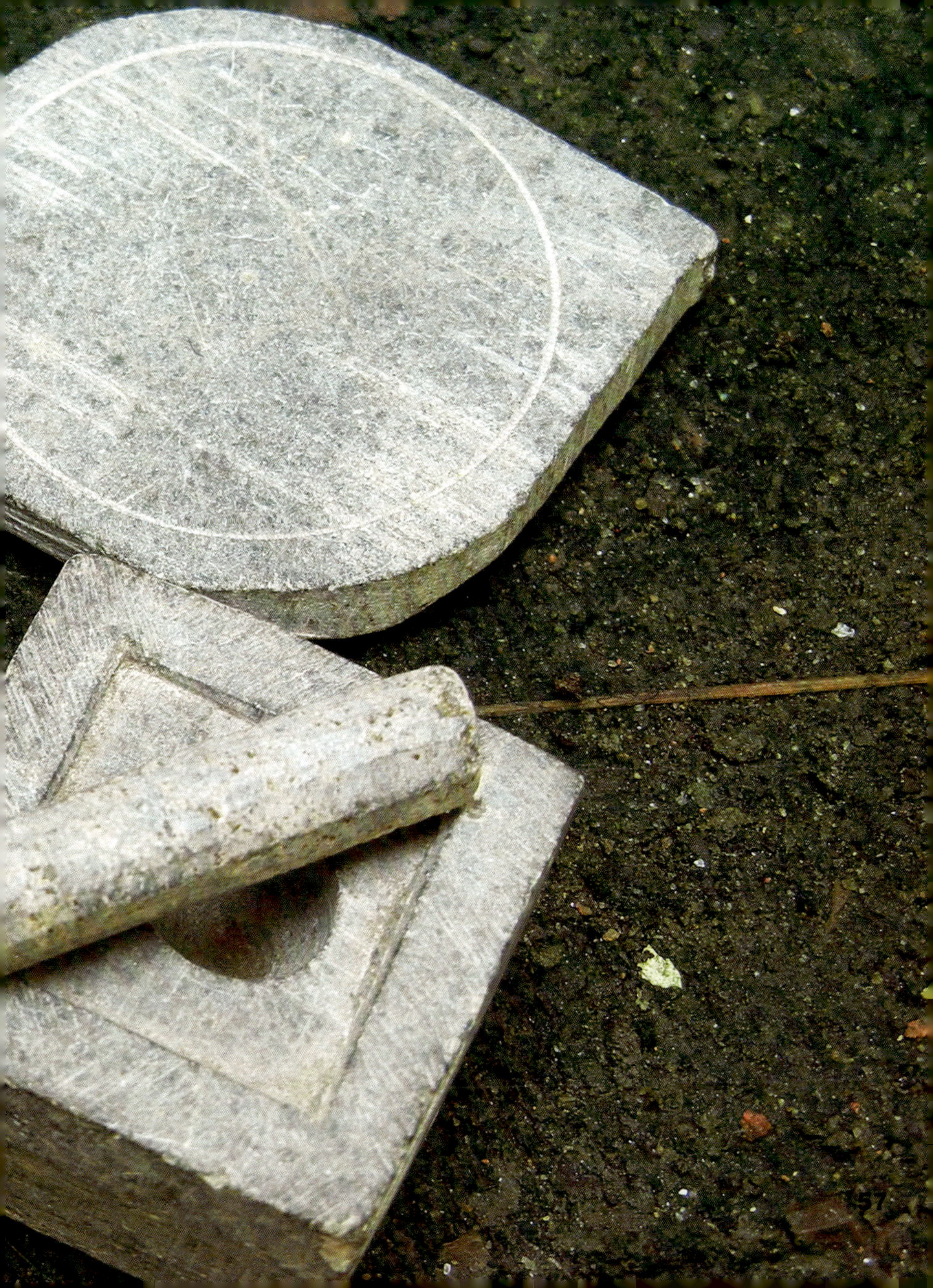

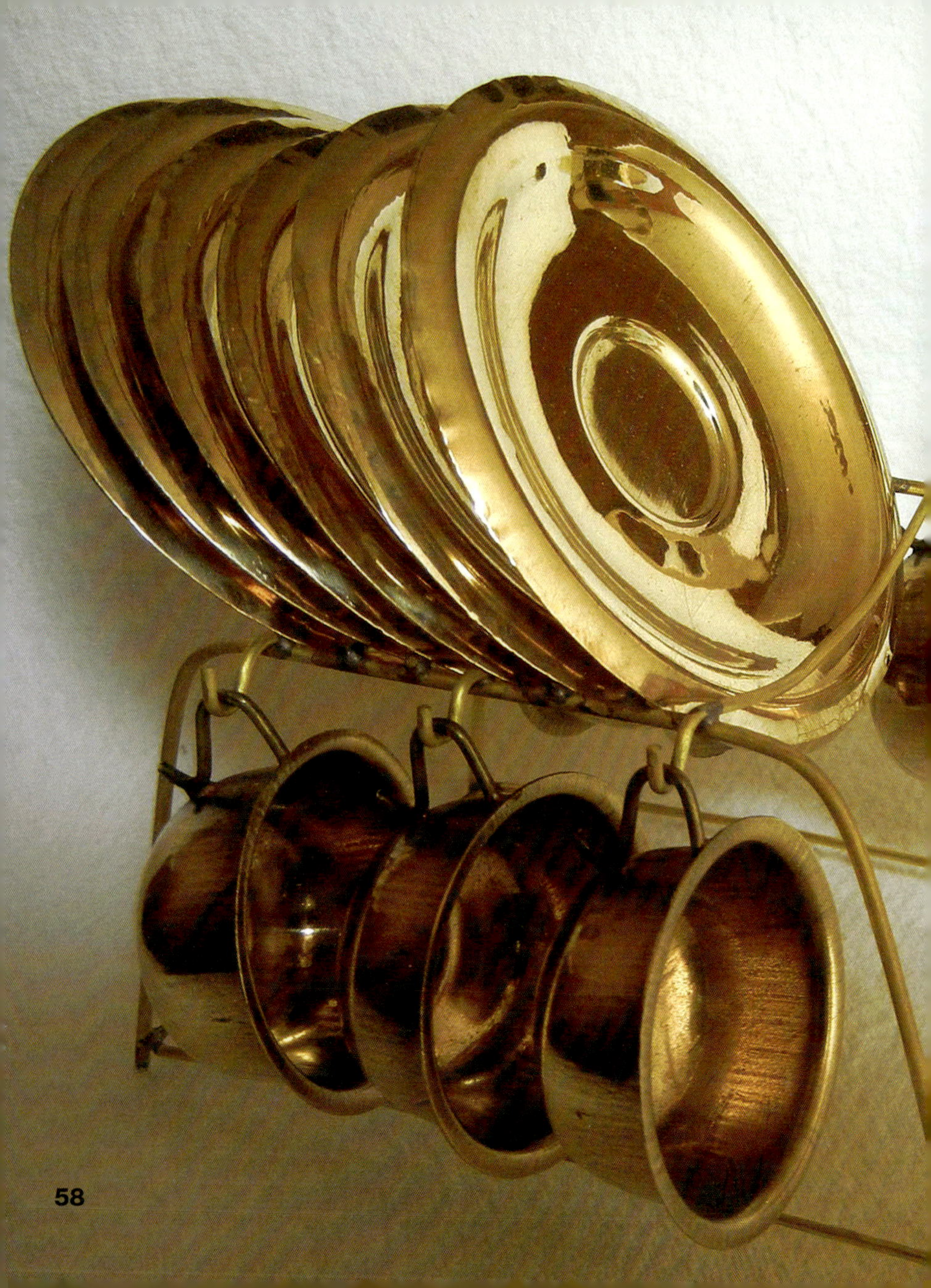

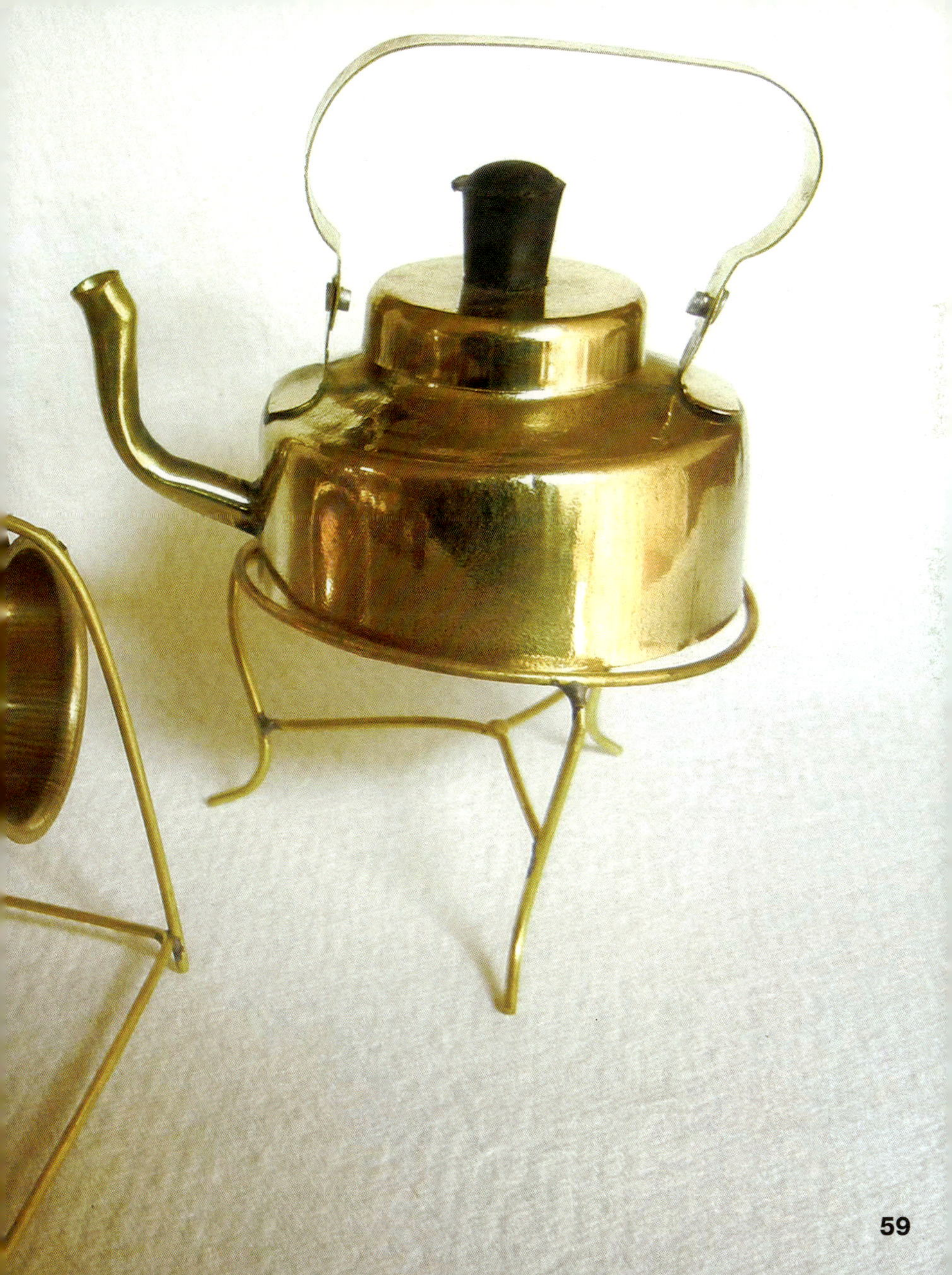

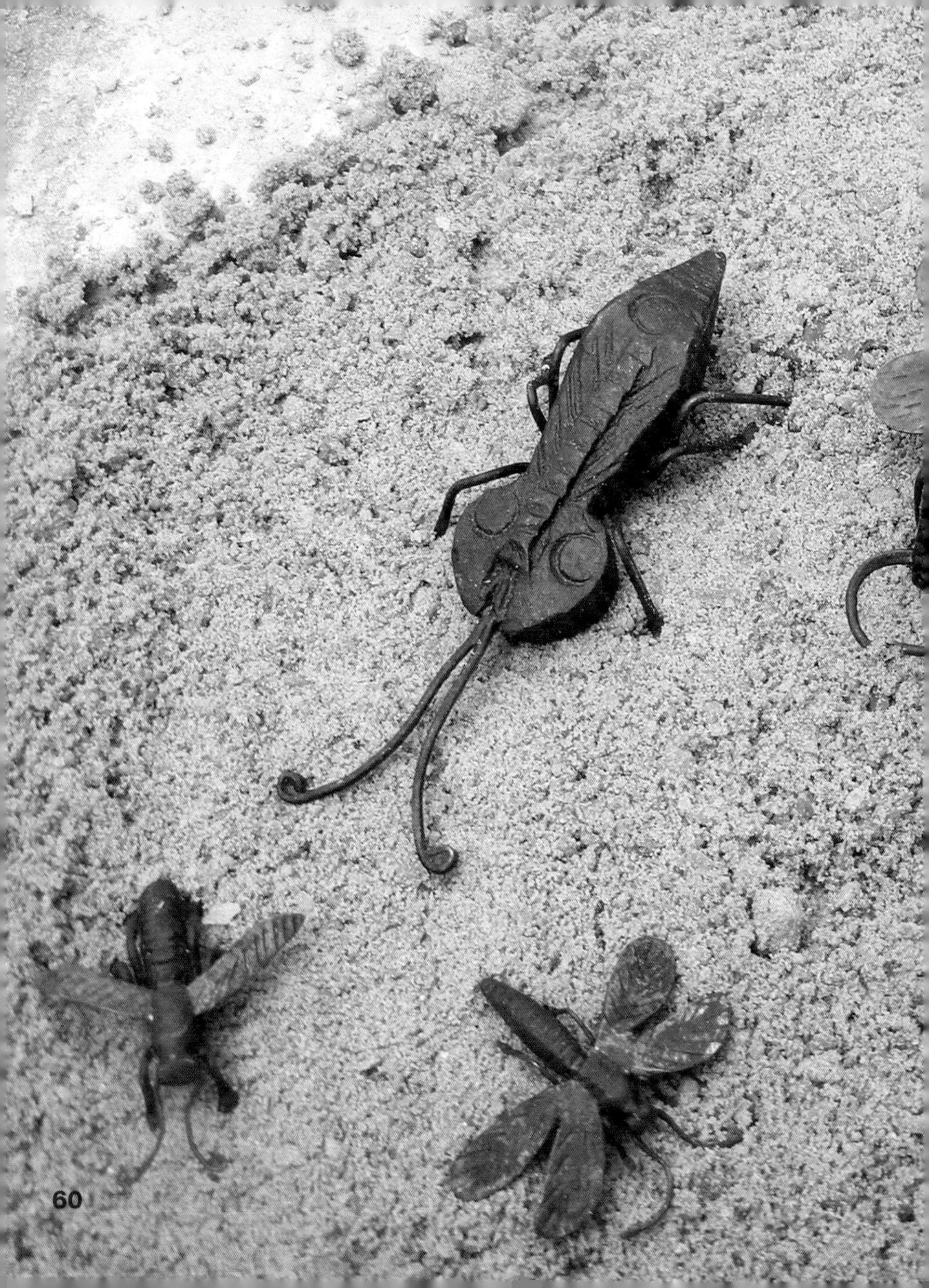

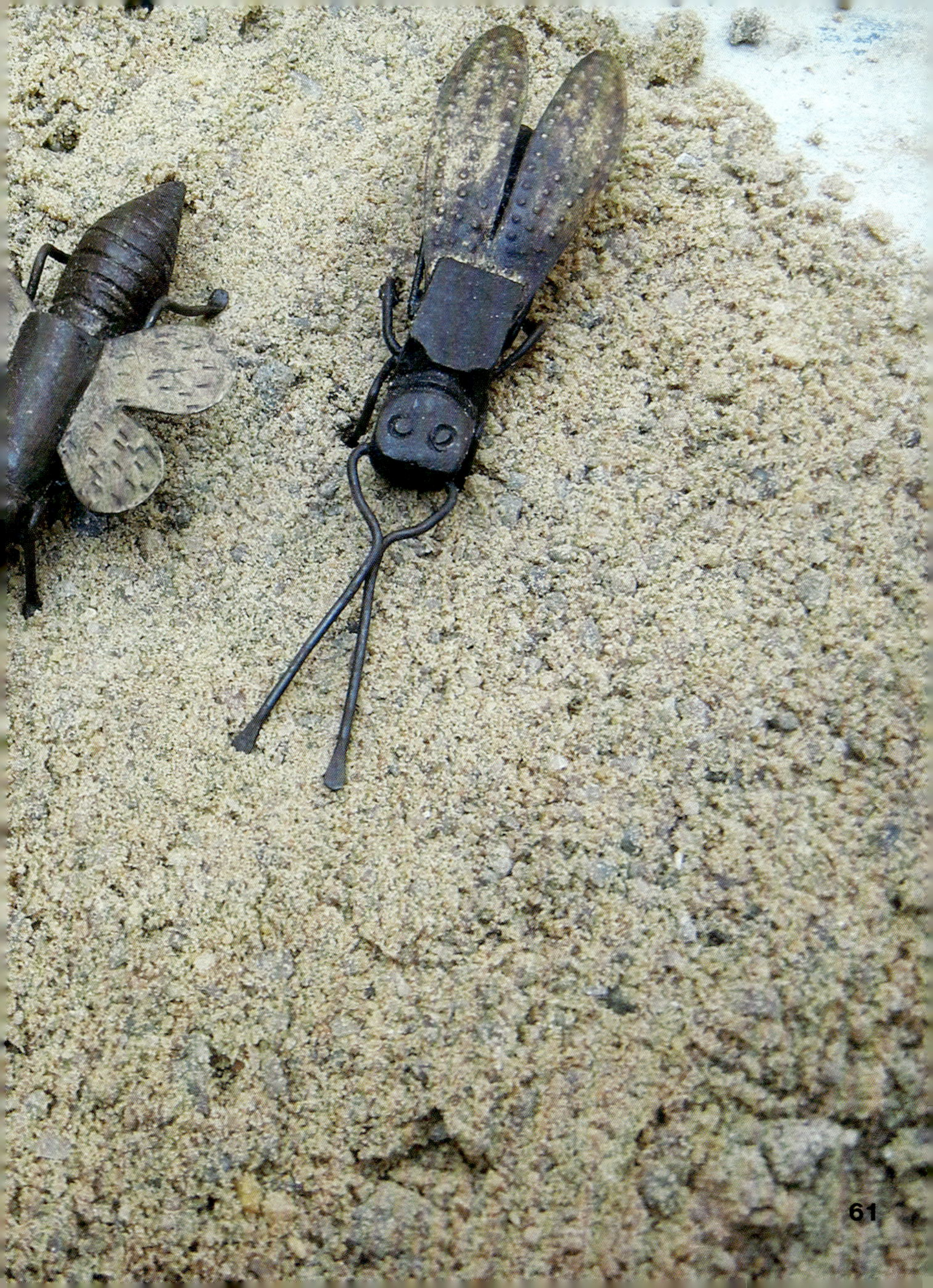

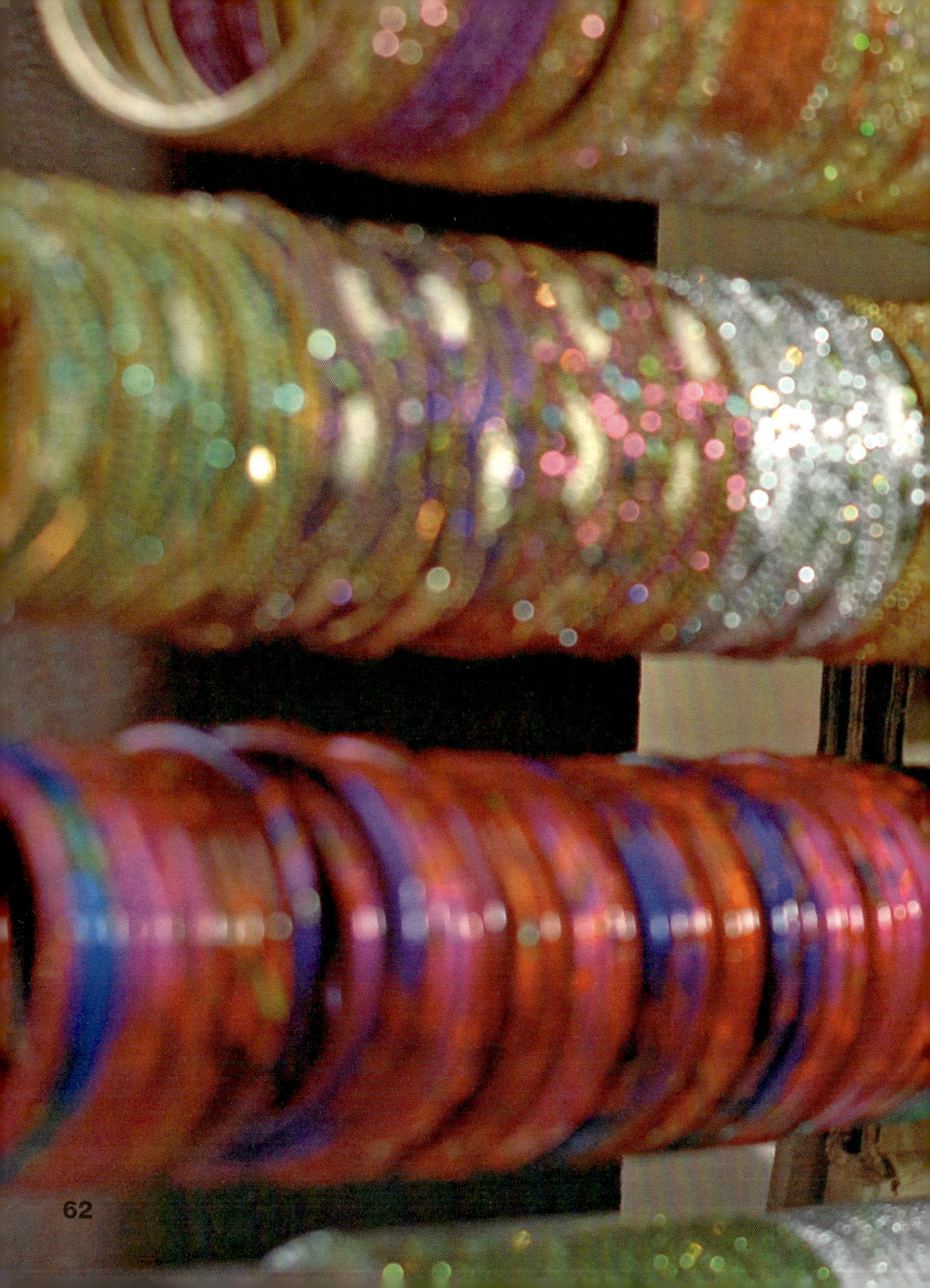

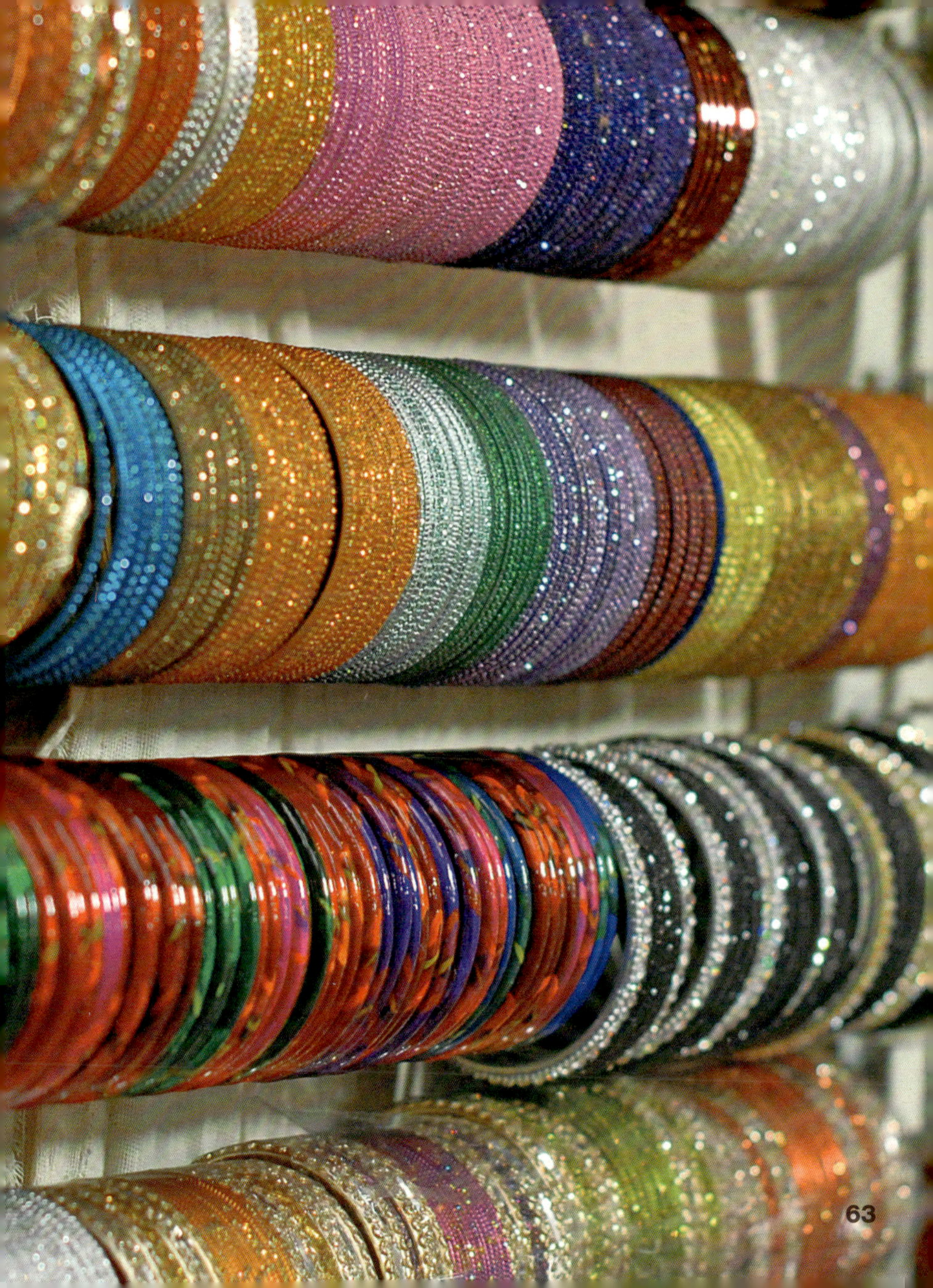

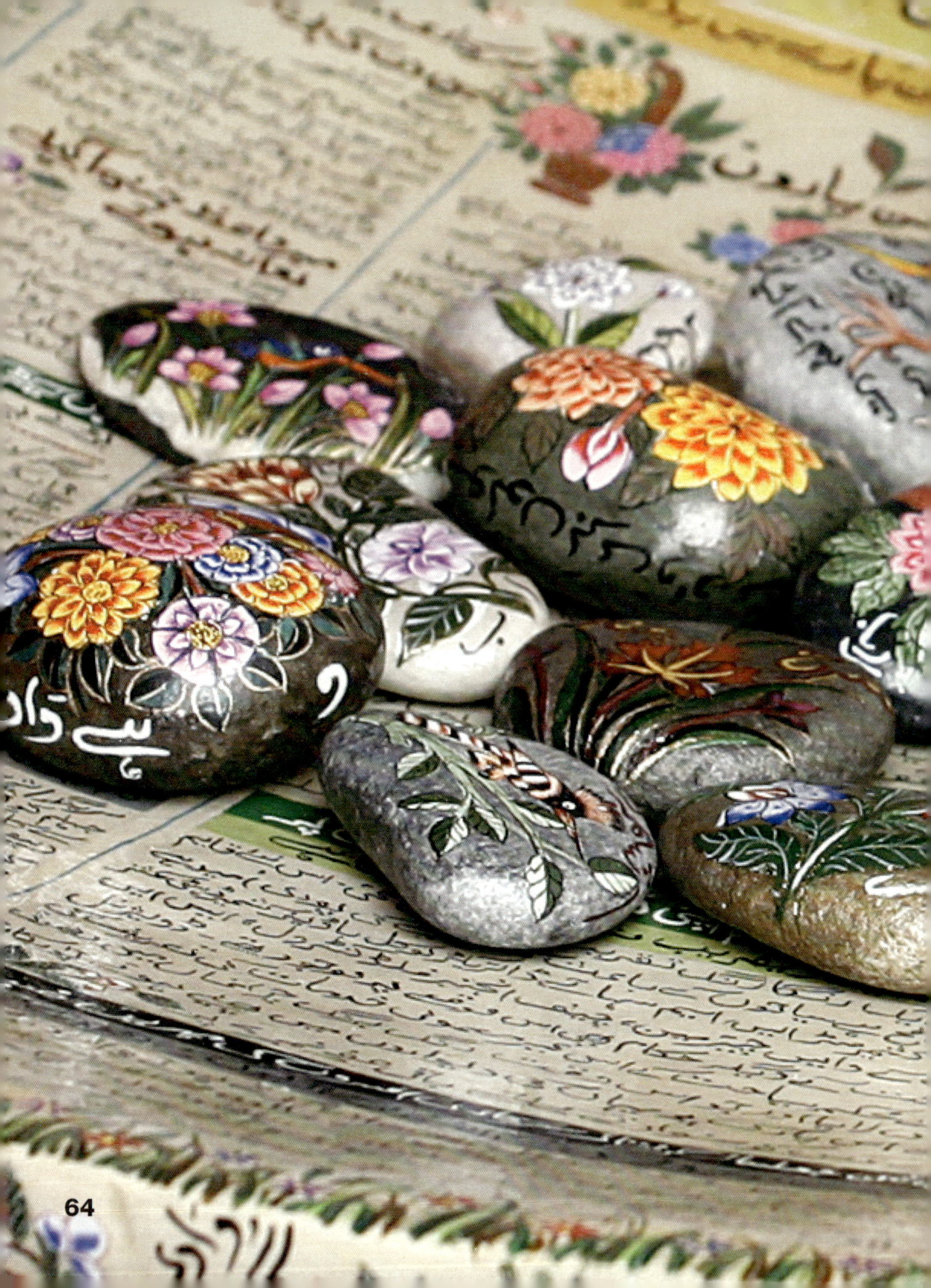

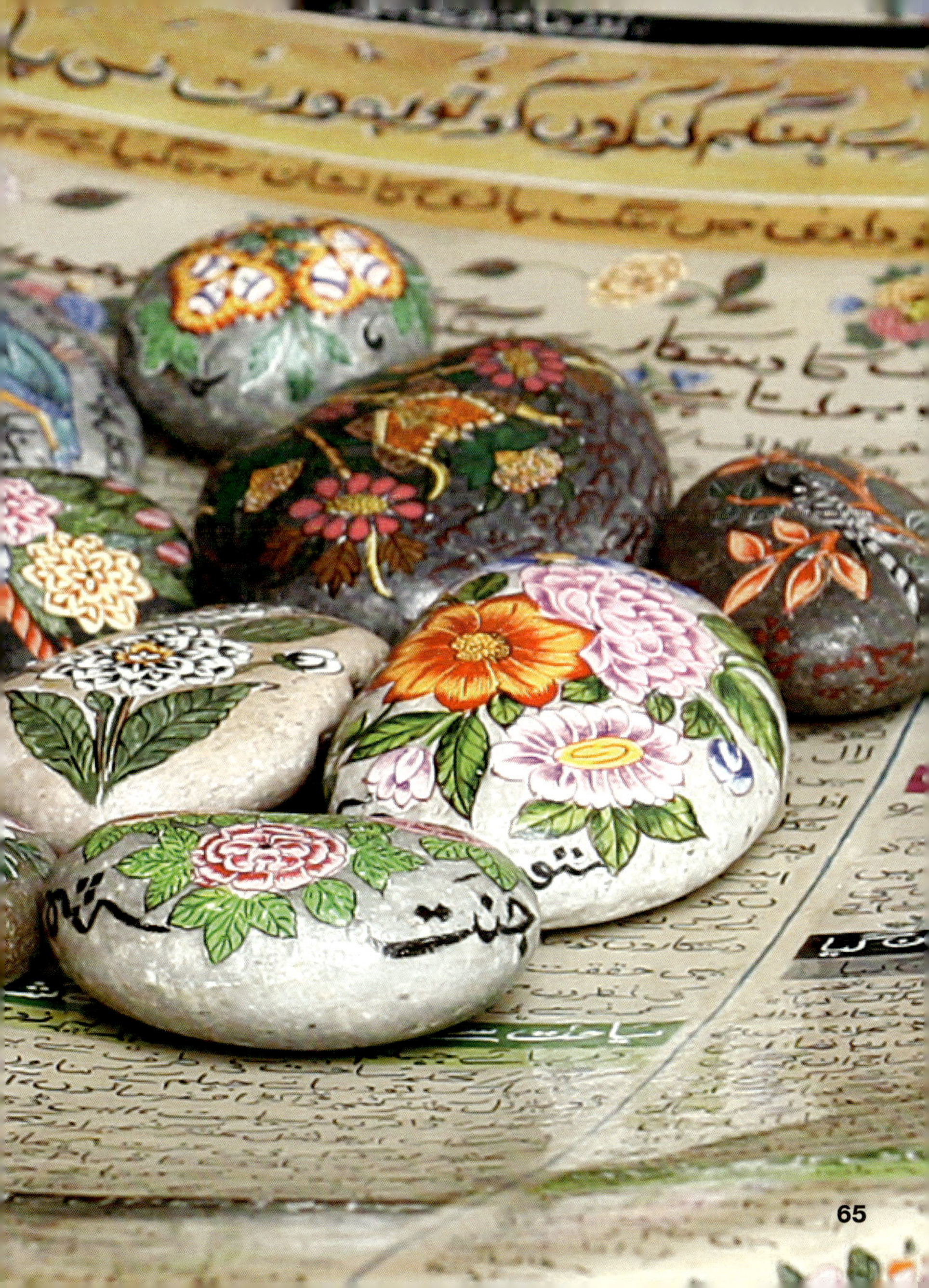

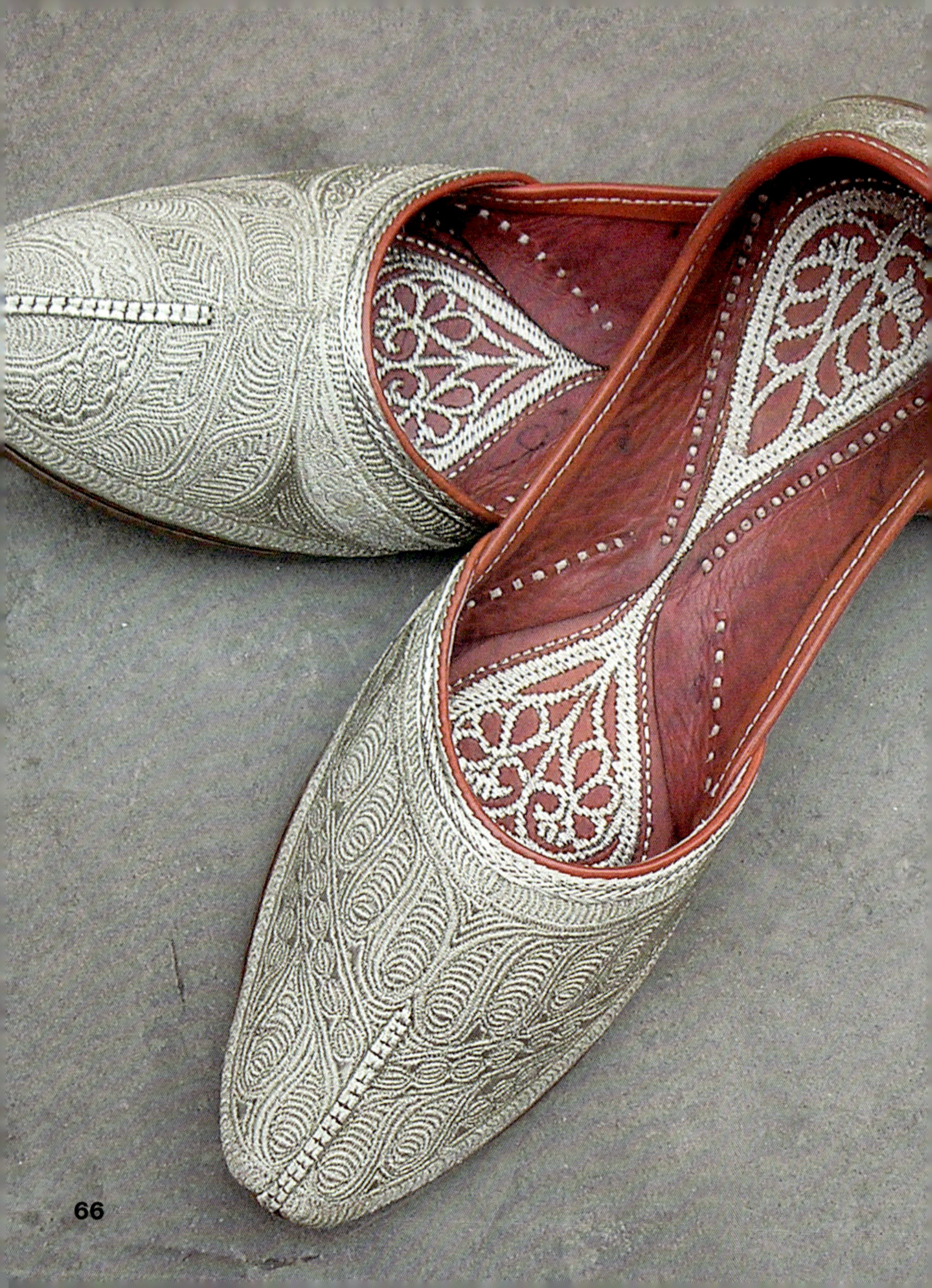

Hand craftsmanship, if it be alive, justifies itself at any time as an intimate expression of the spirit of man. Such work is an end in itself and not a means to an end. If, however, it ceases to serve a functional need, it runs the risk of becoming art for art's sake and untrue to its nature, depending on the sincerity of the craftsman.

~ Soetsu Yanagi
The Unknown Craftsman

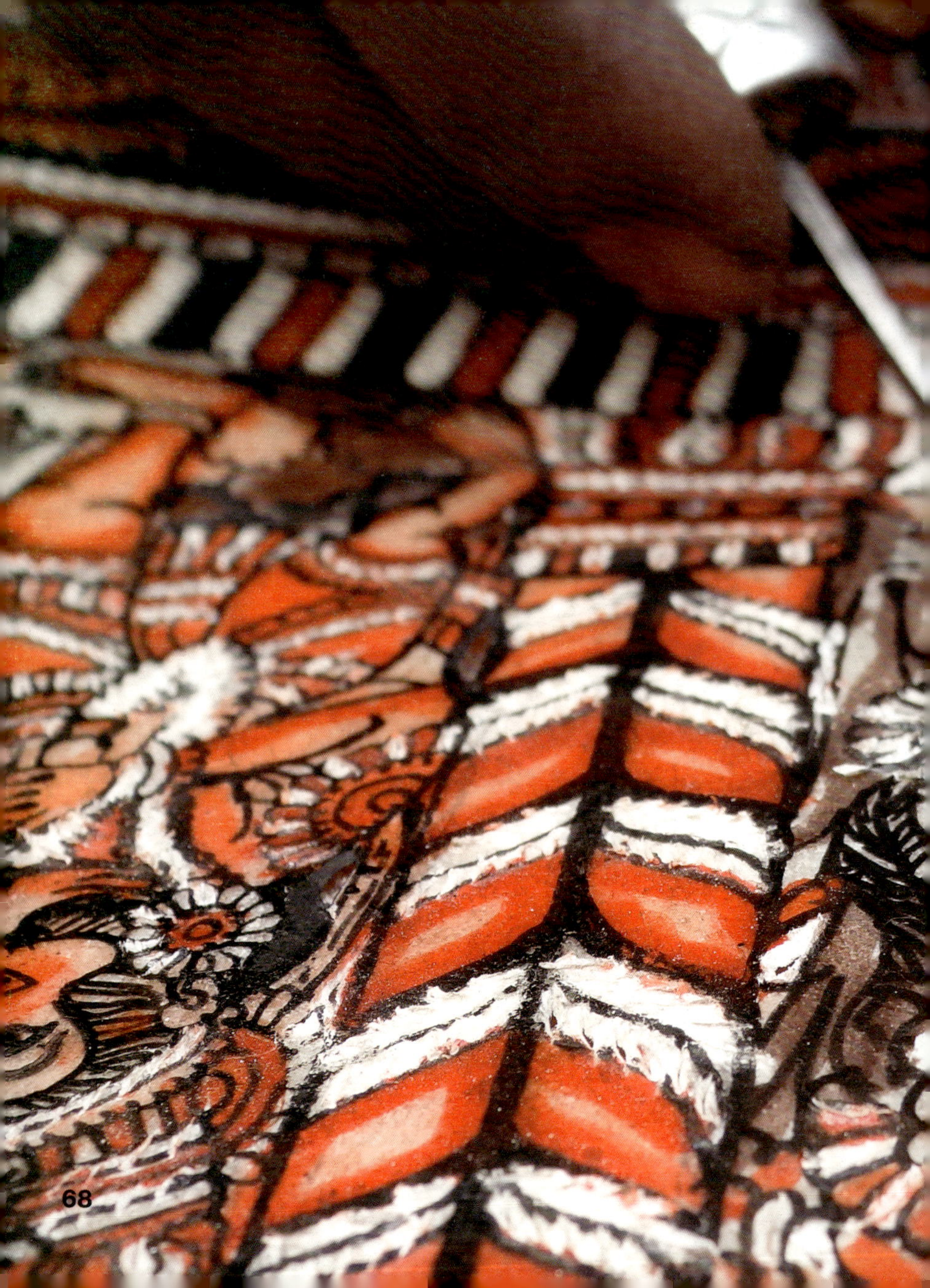

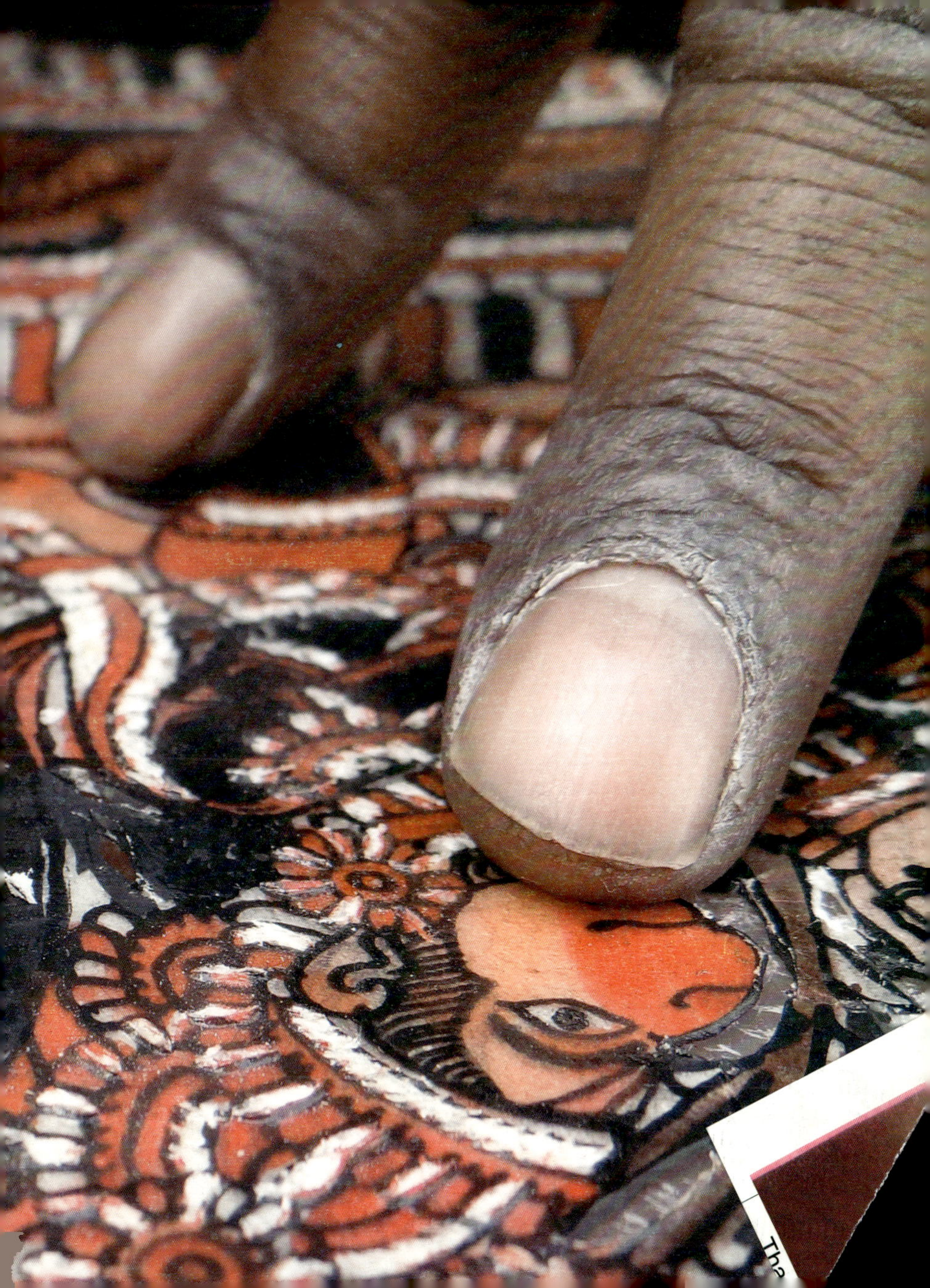

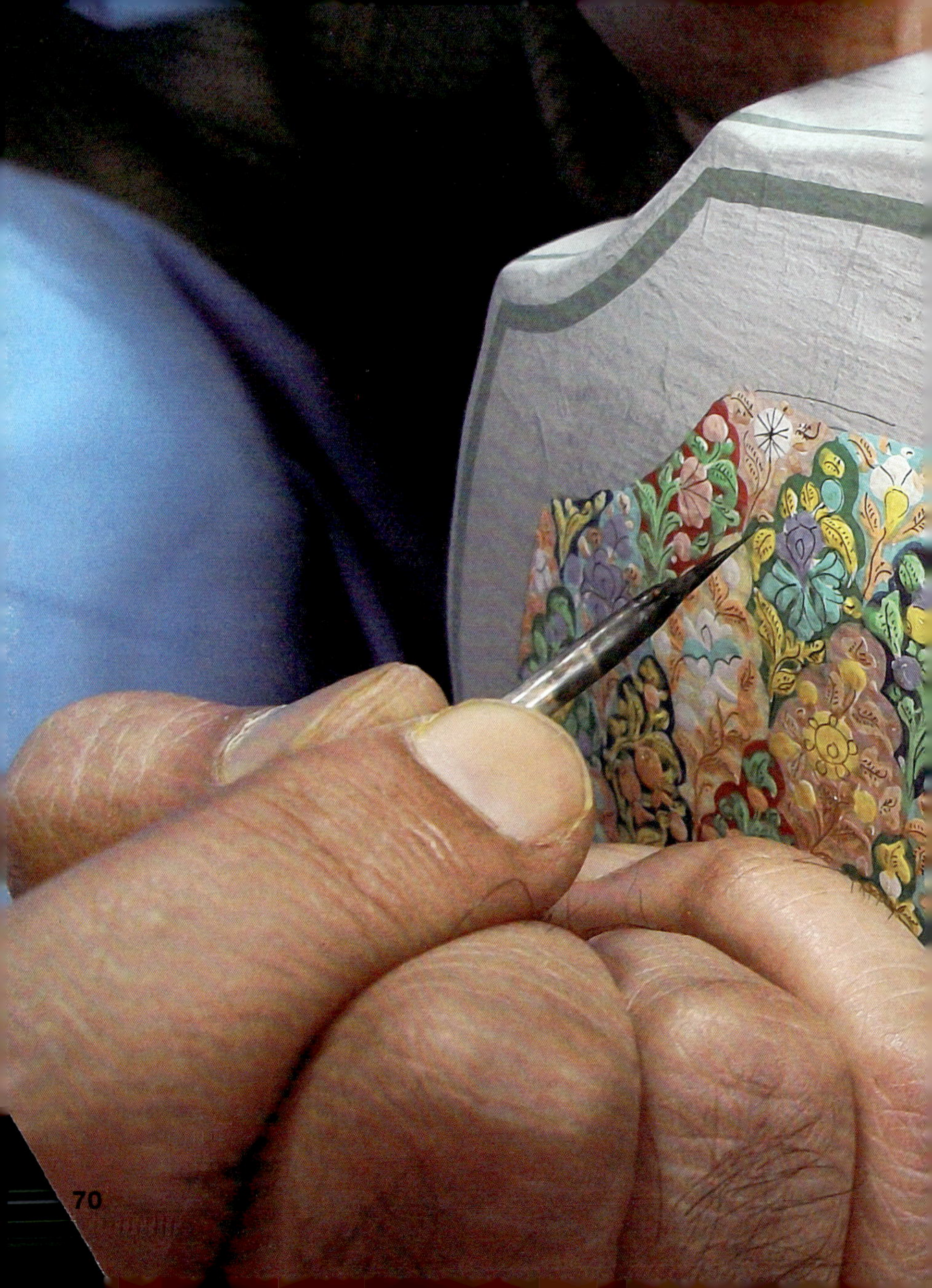

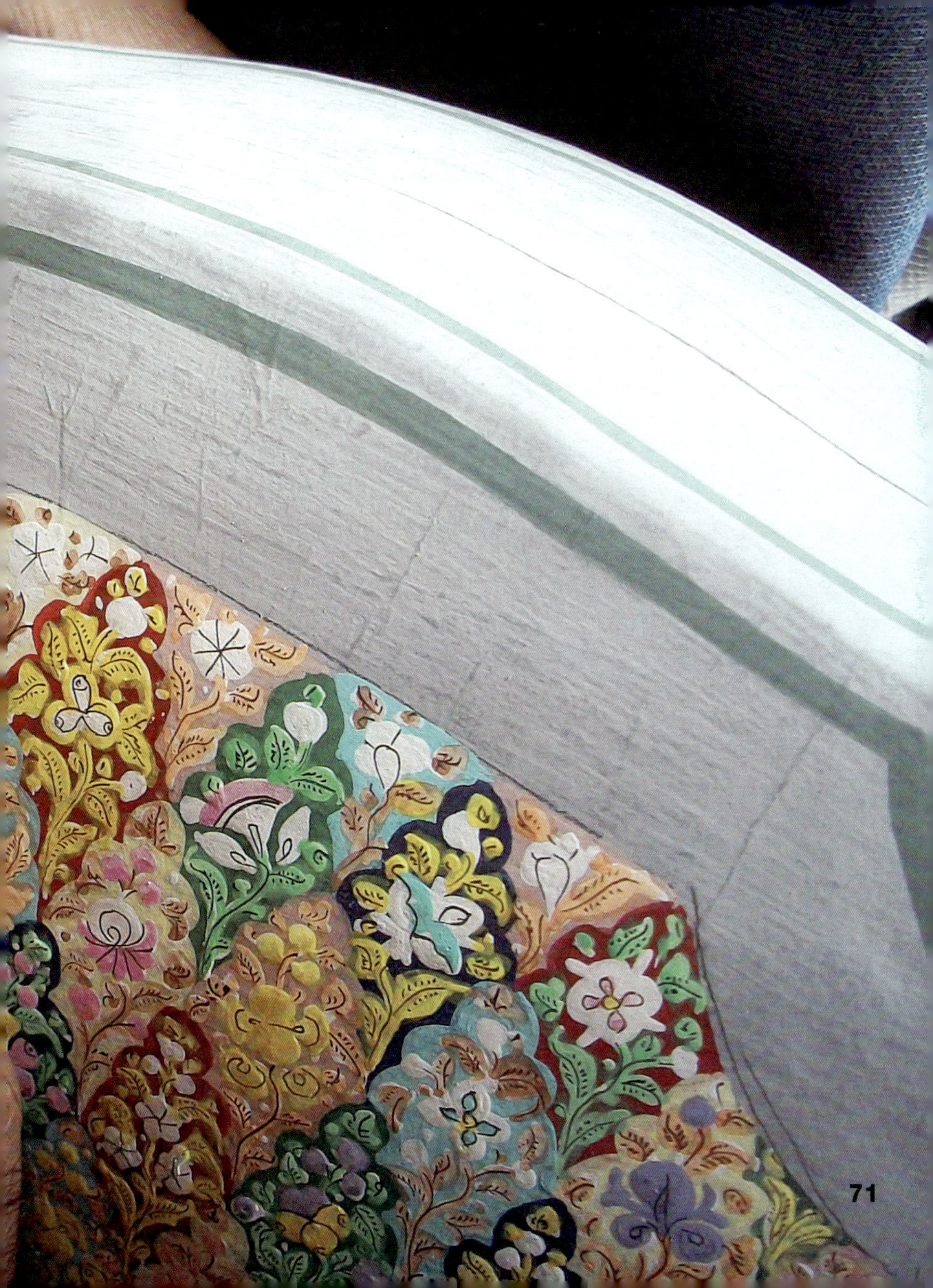

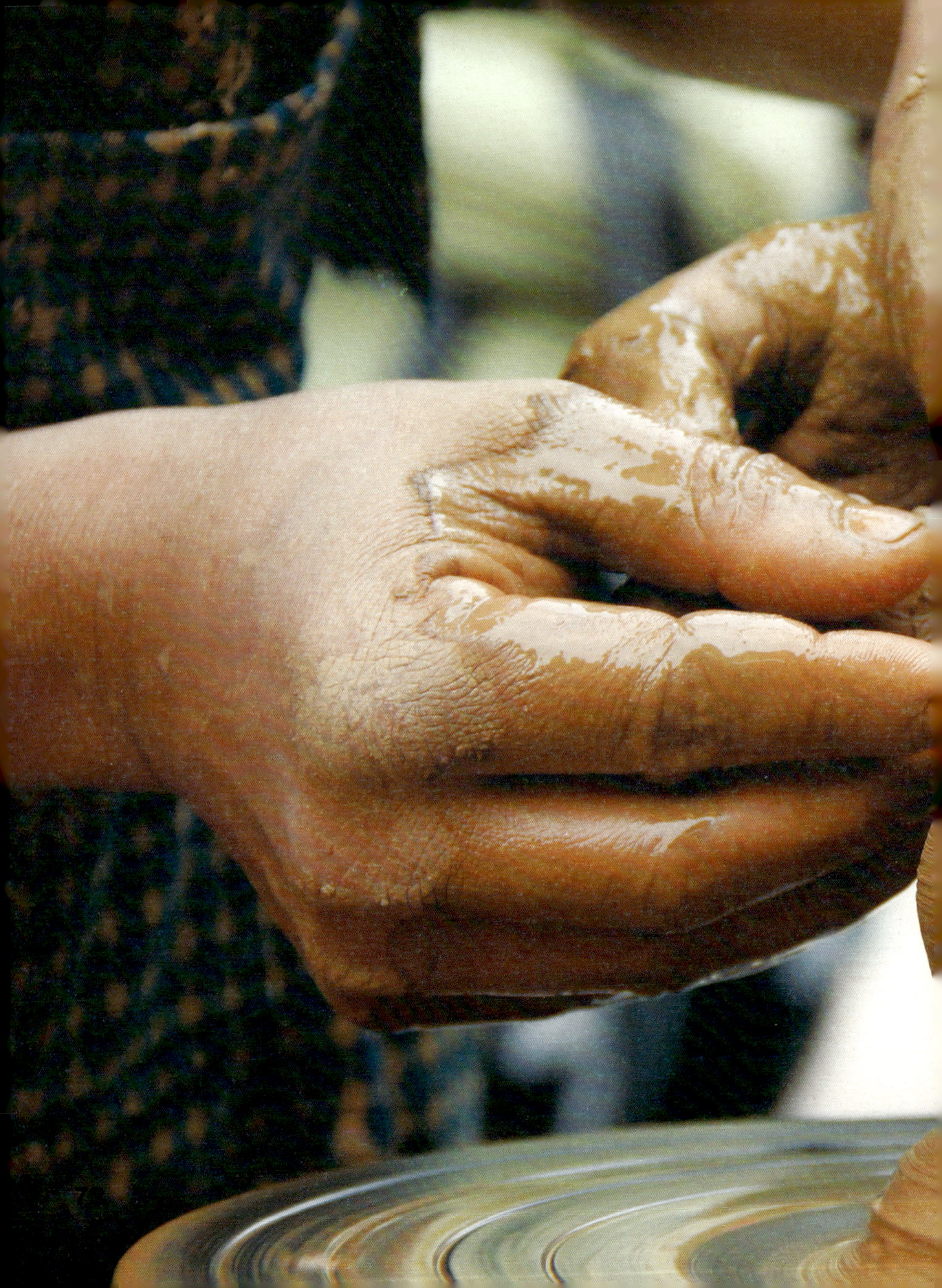

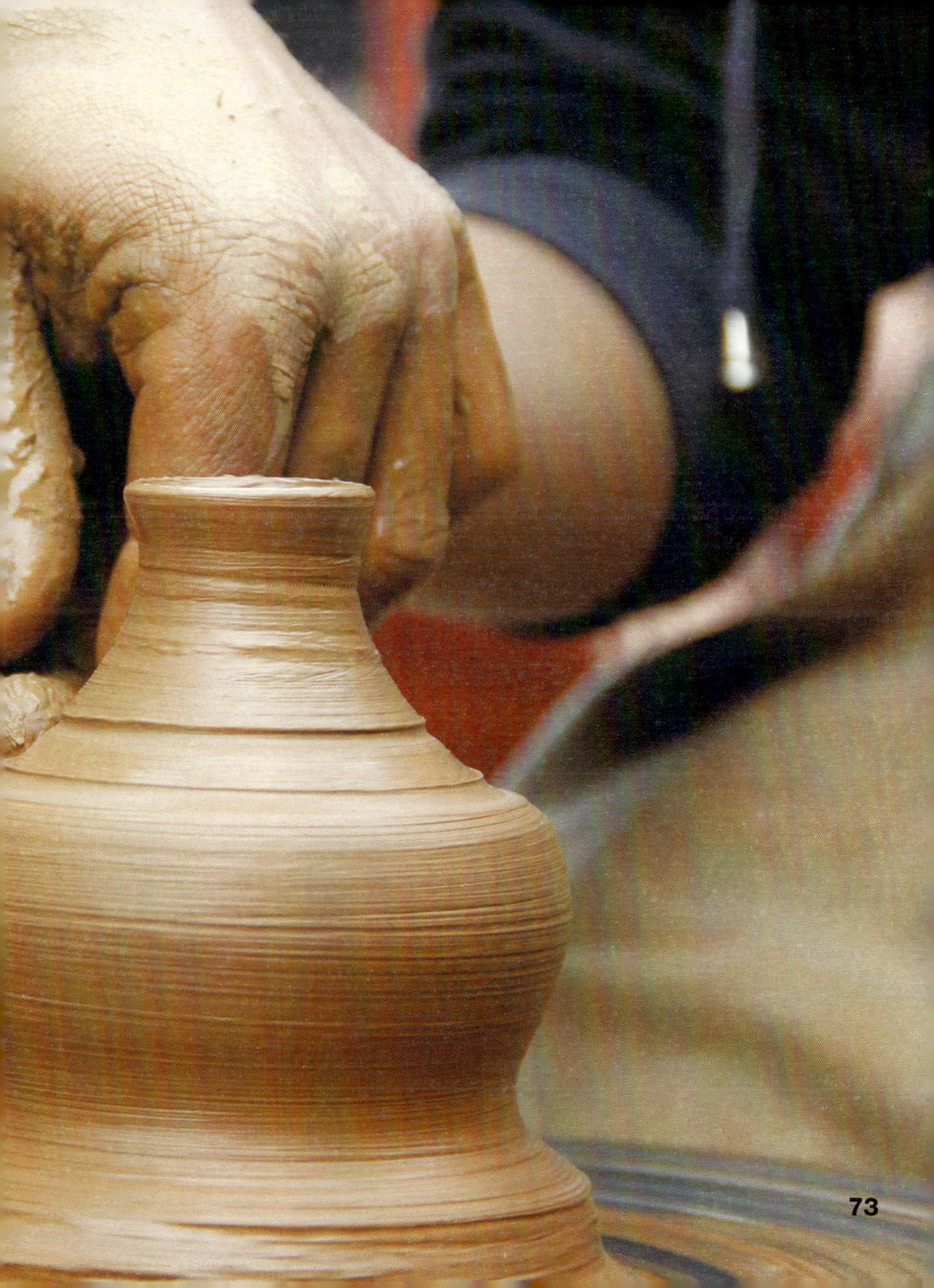

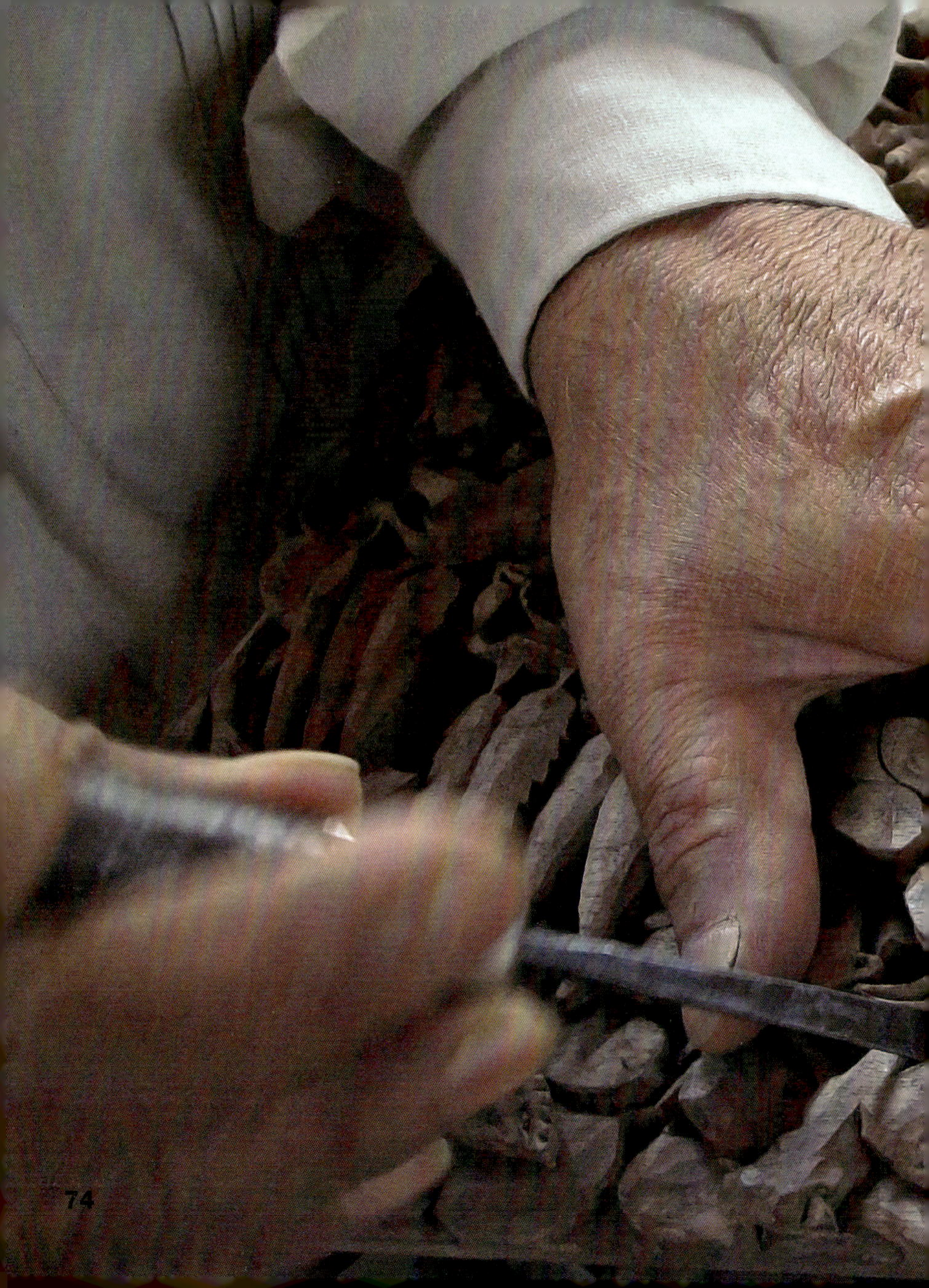

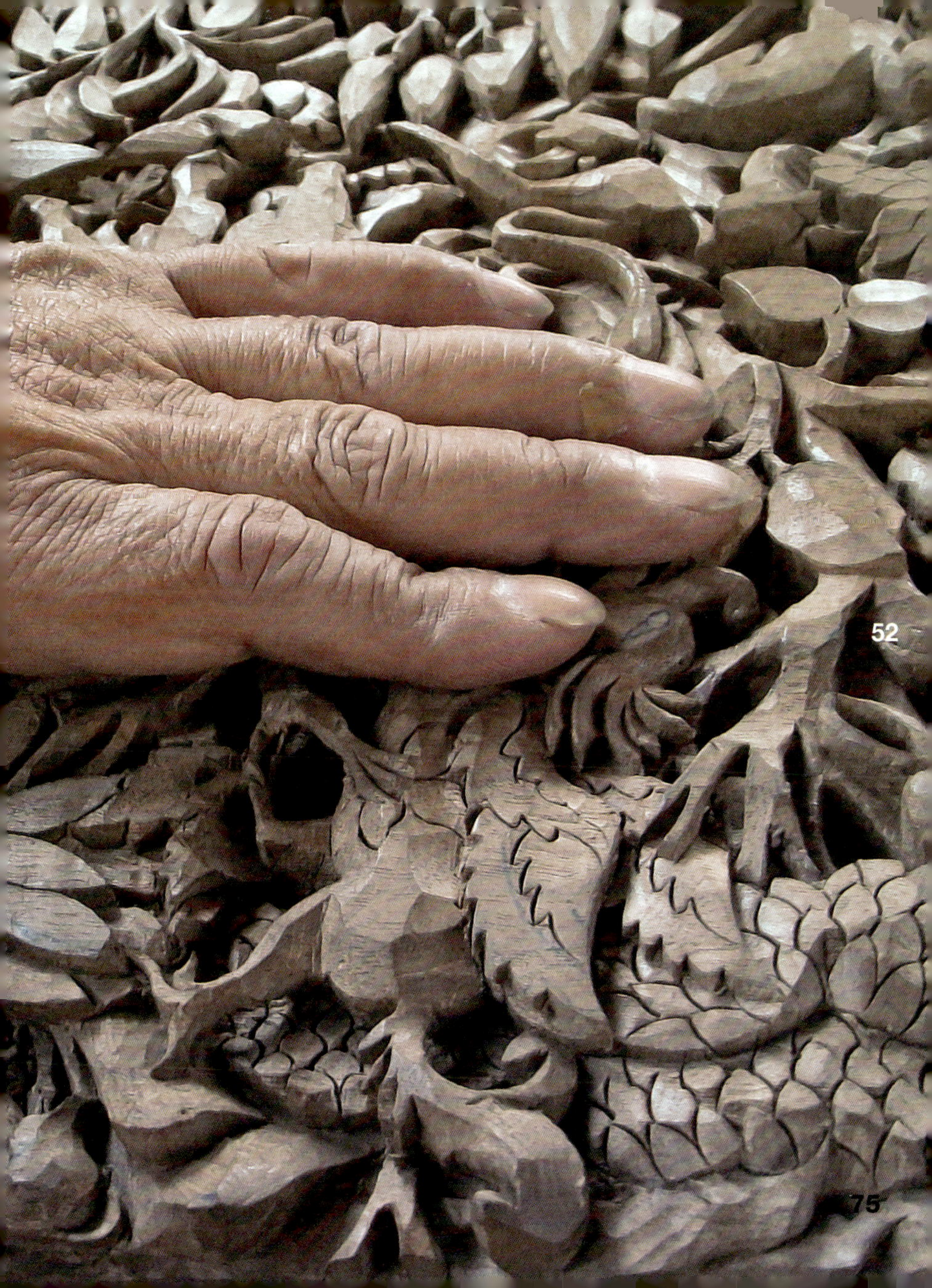

52

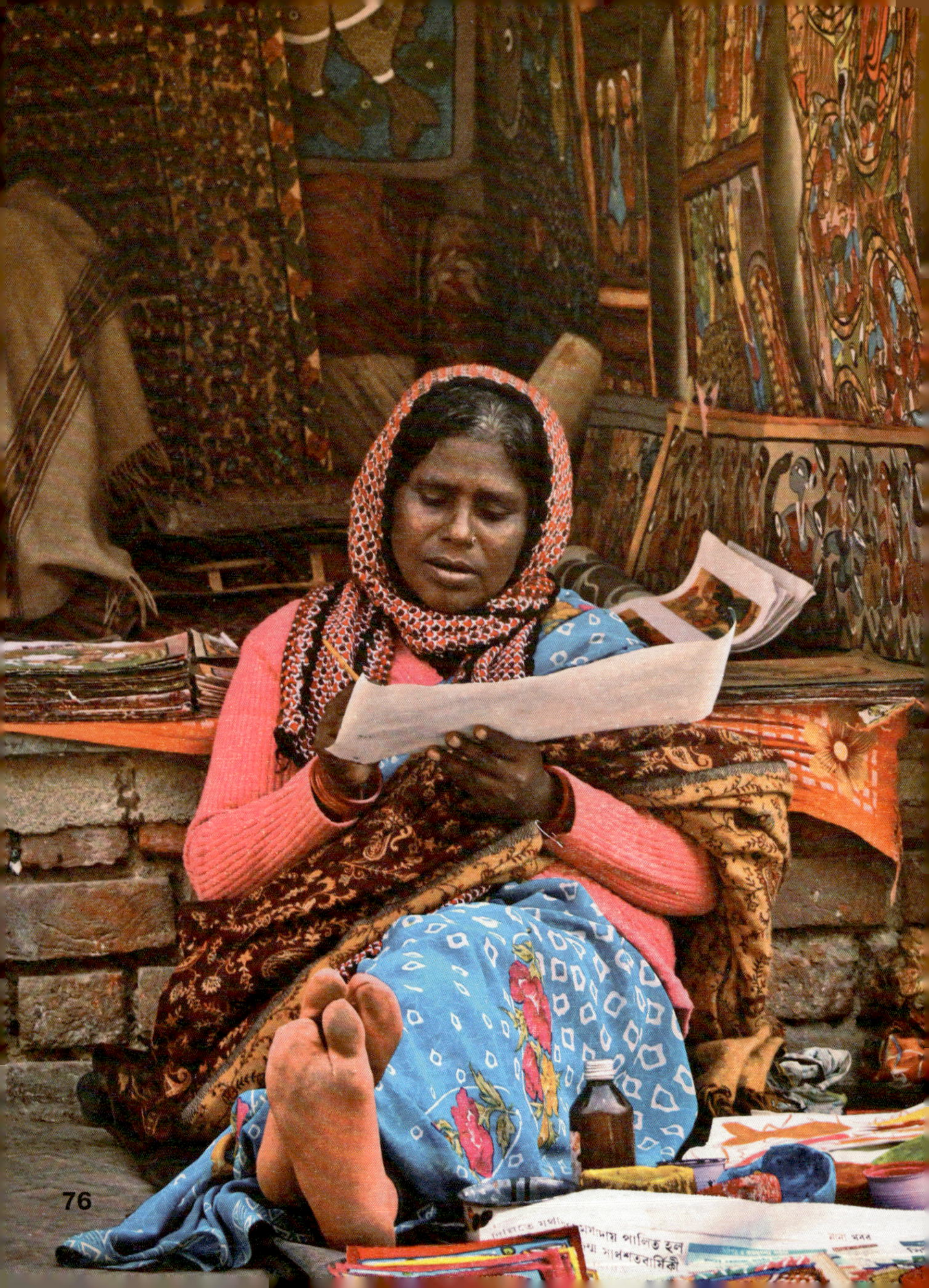
পালিত হল

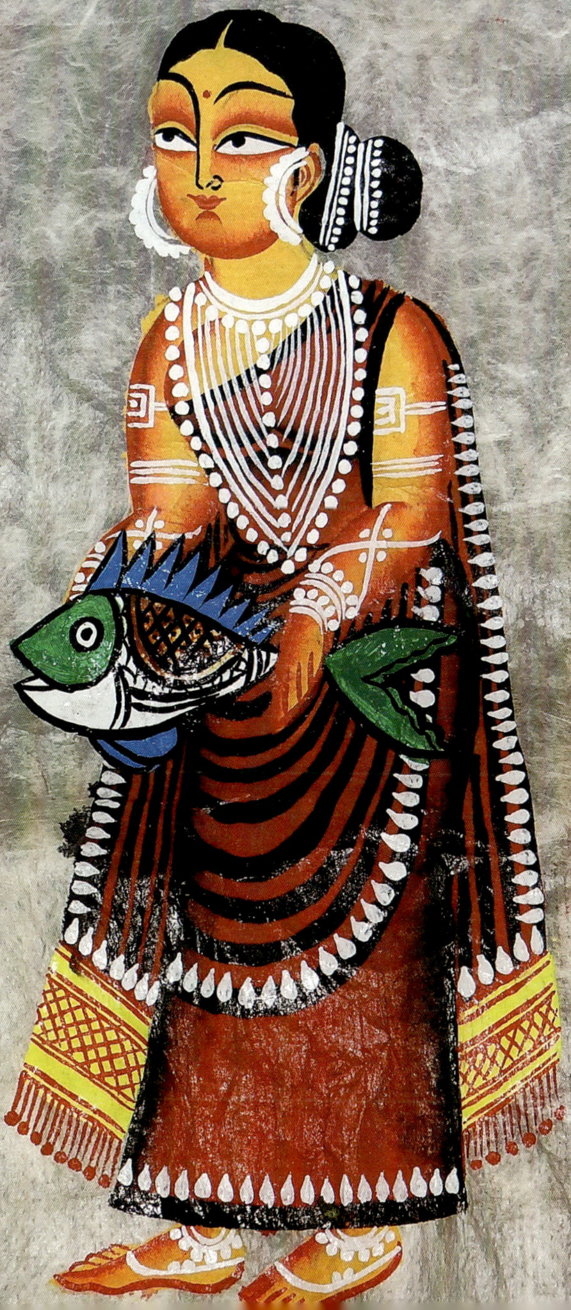

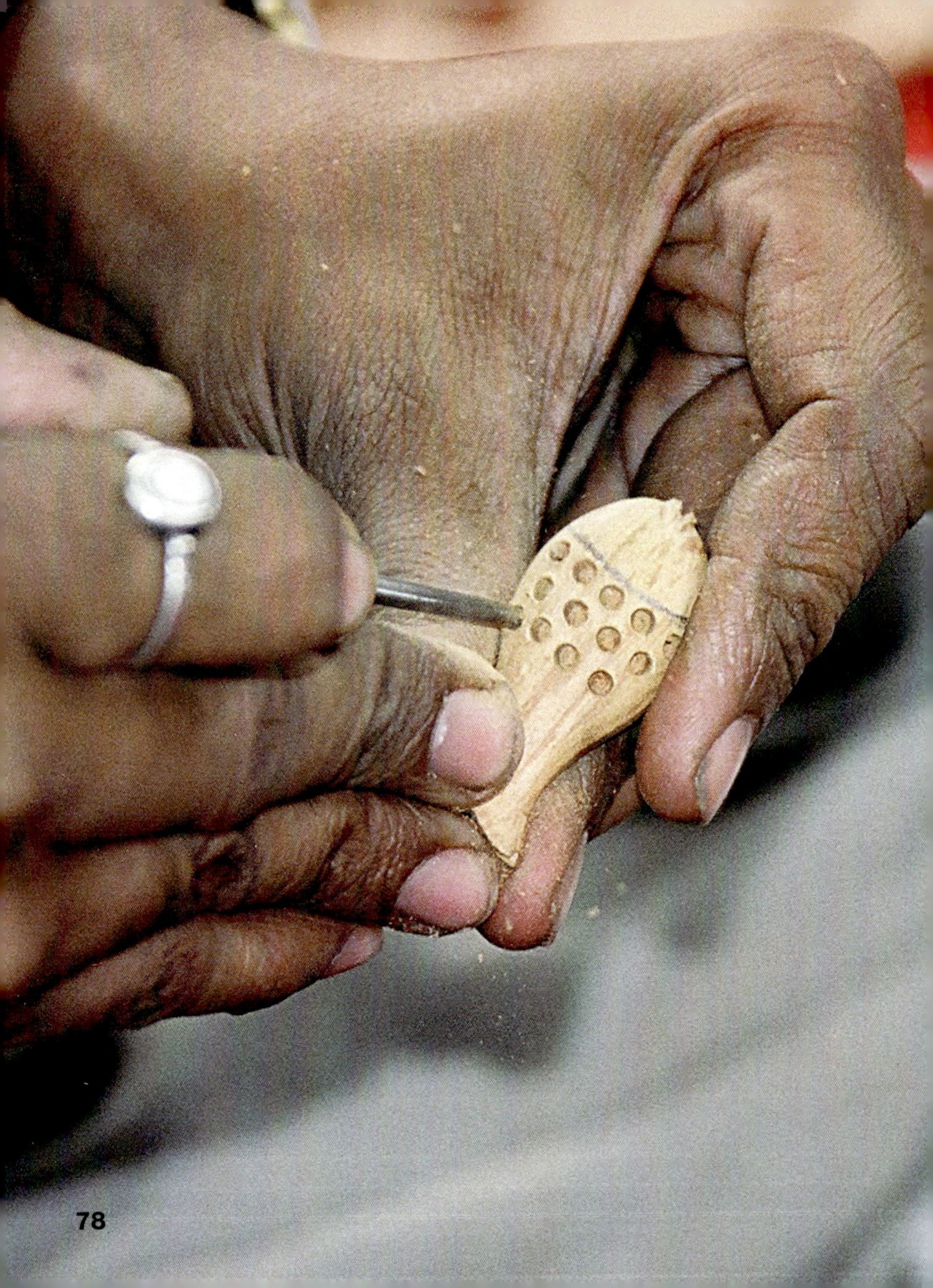

The chief characteristic of handcrafts is that they maintain by their very nature a direct link with the human heart, so that the work always partakes of a human quality.

~ Soetsu Yanagi
The Unknown Craftsman

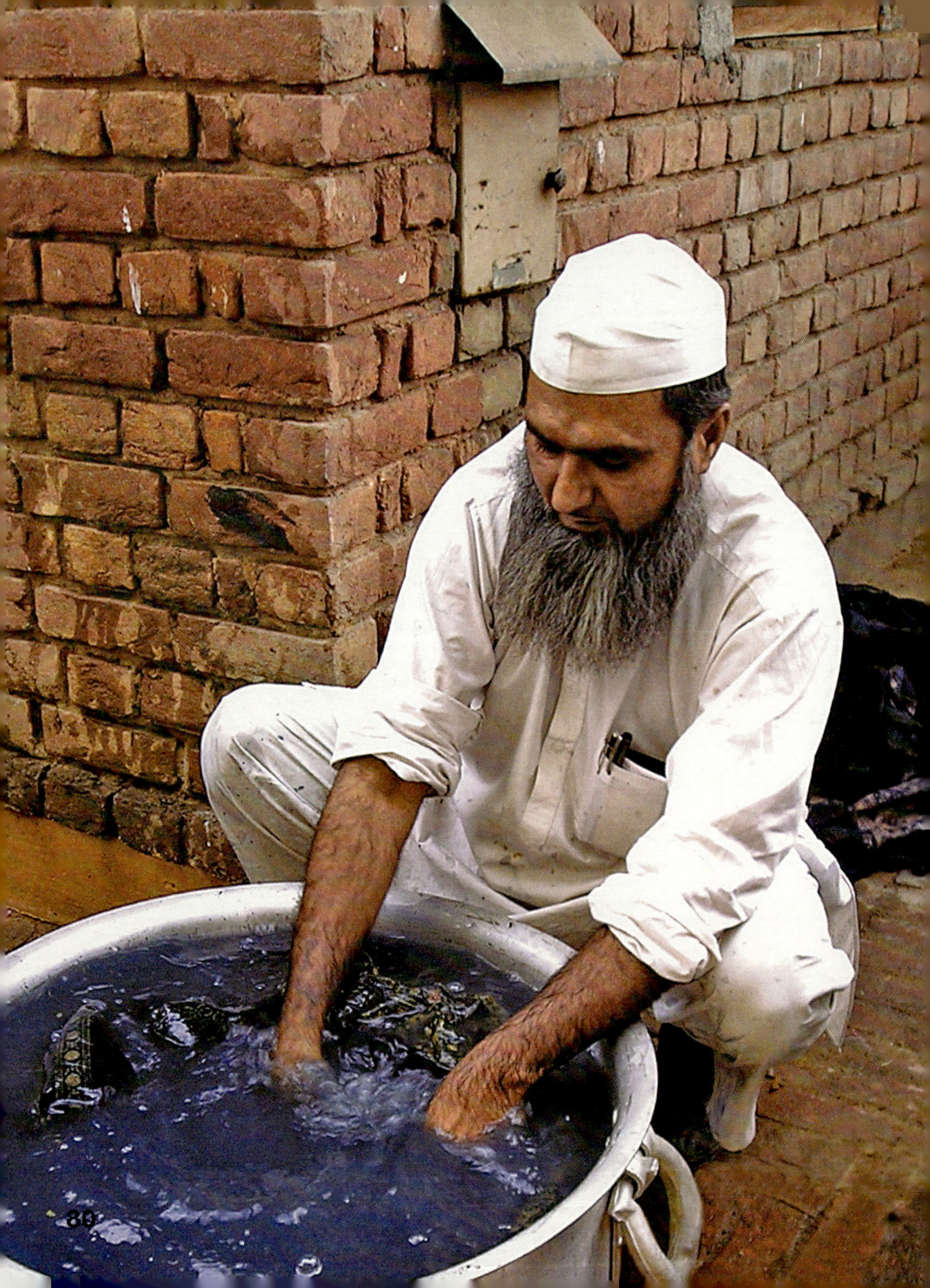

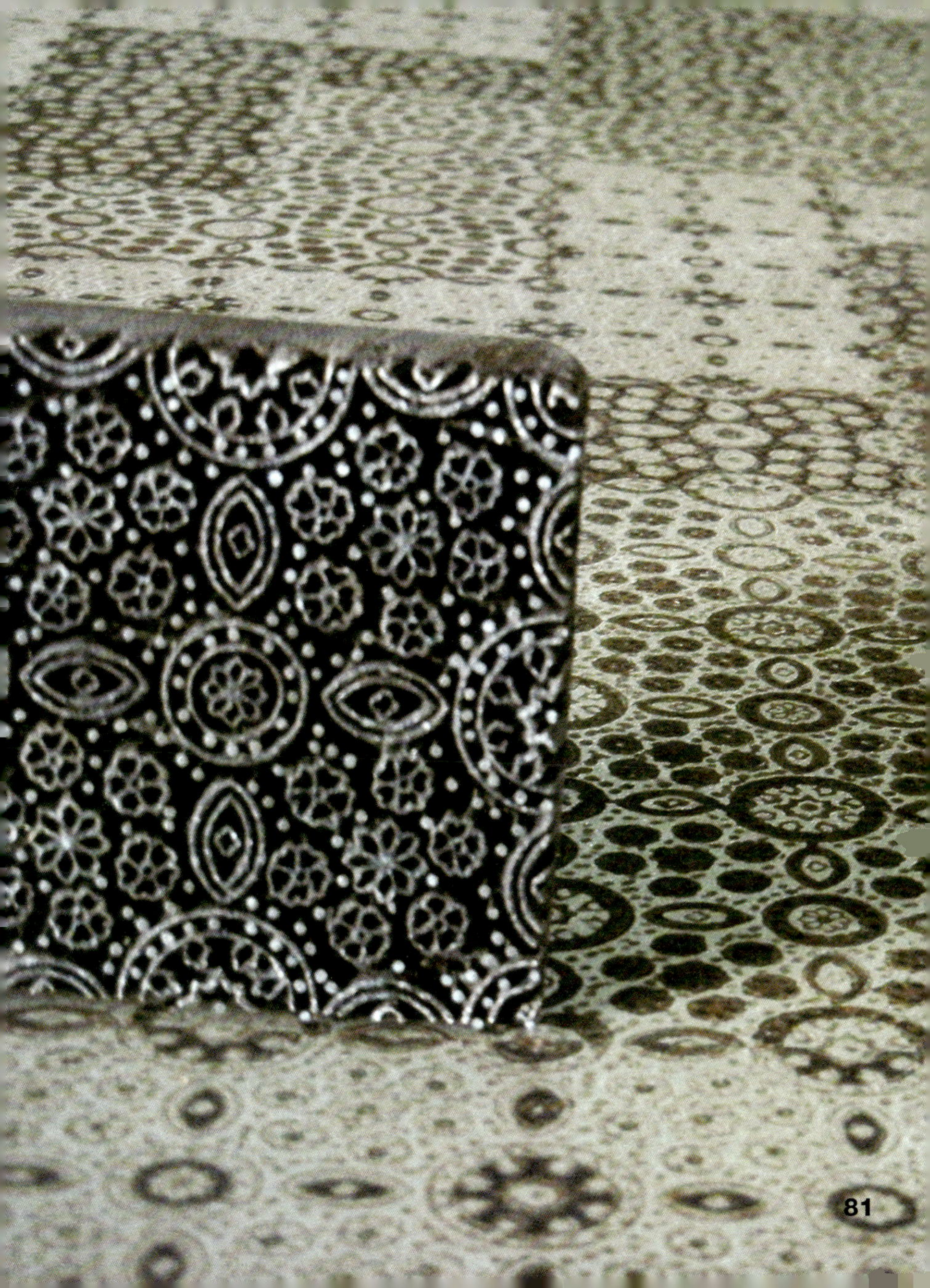

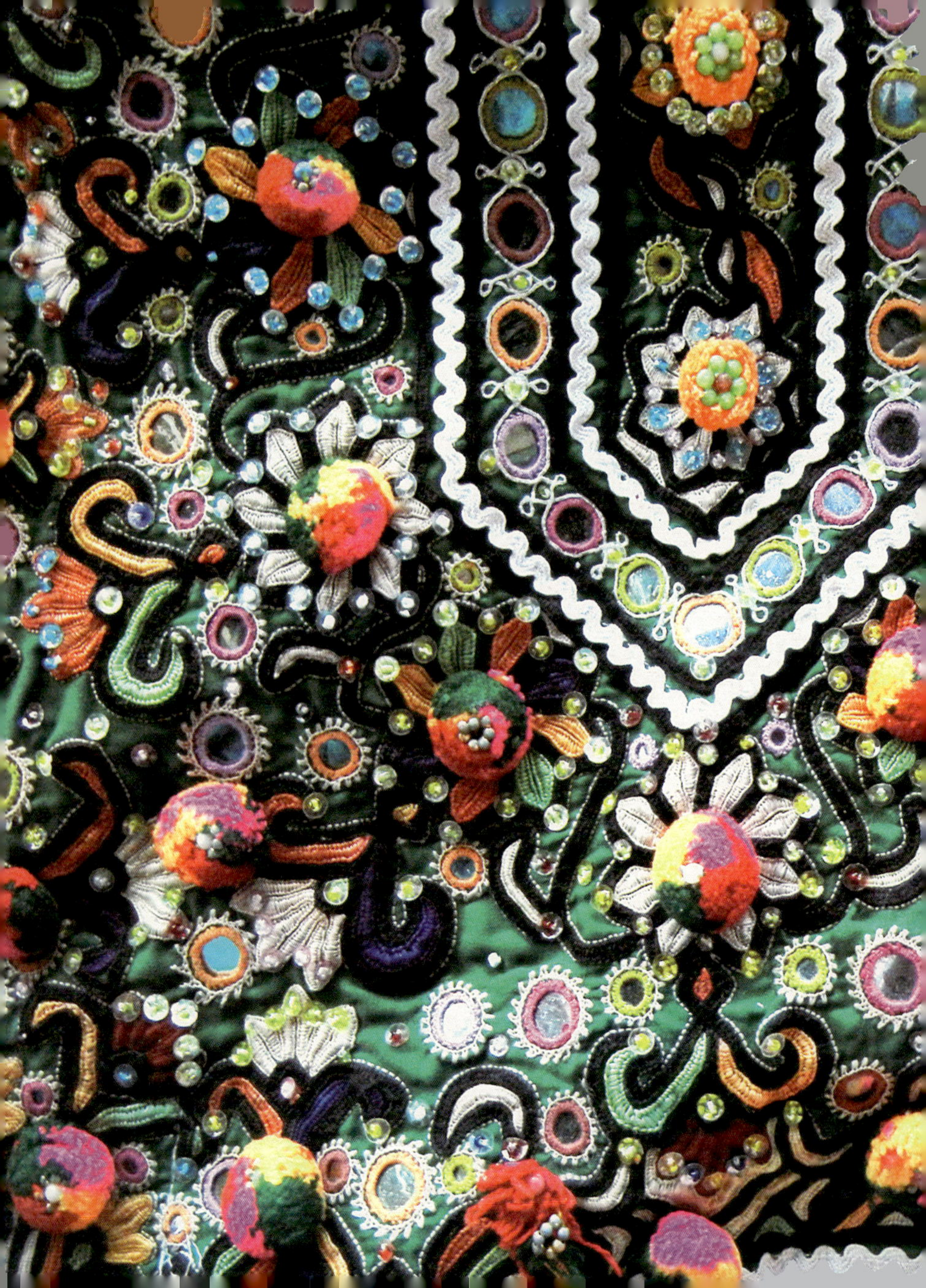

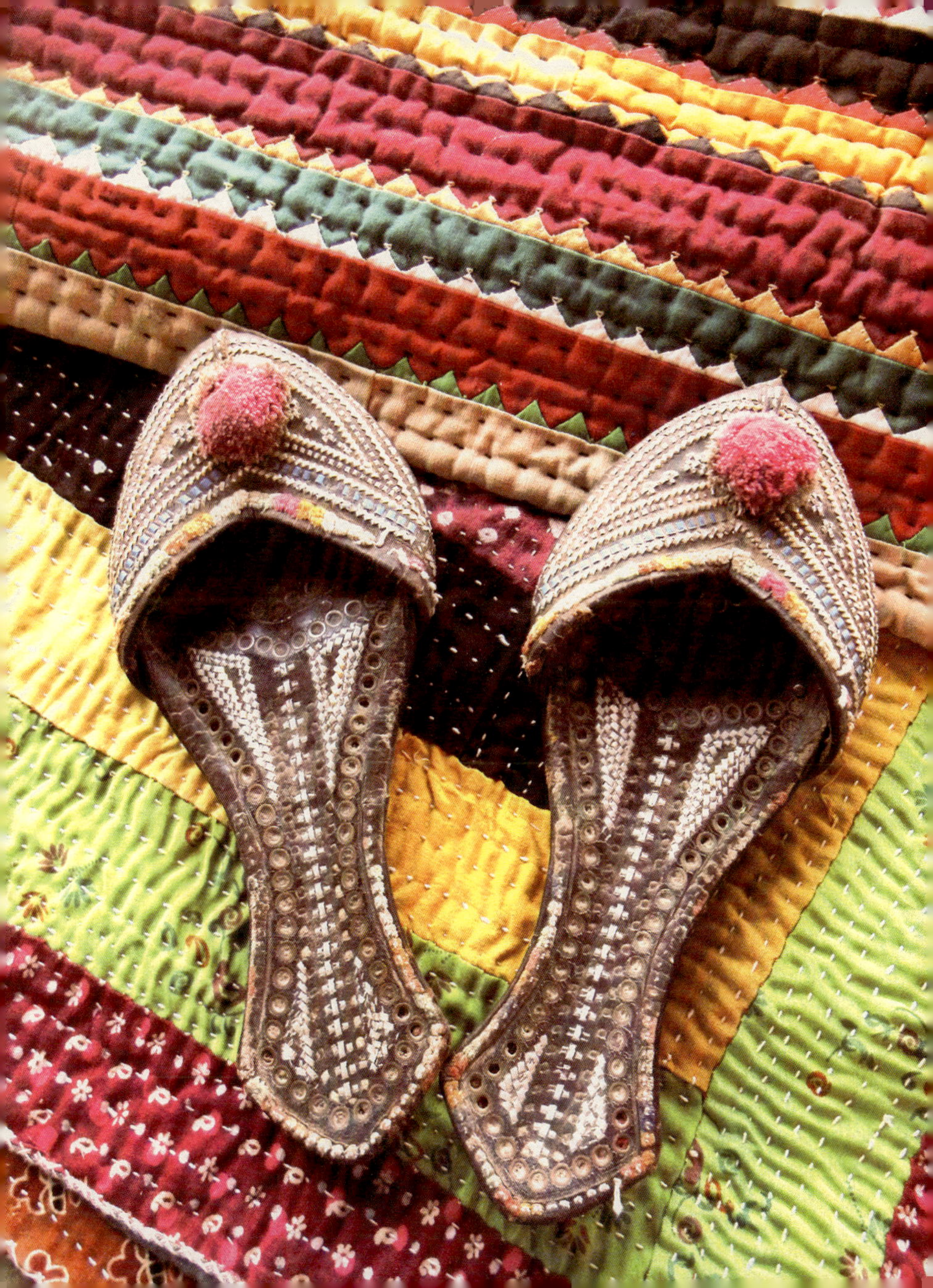

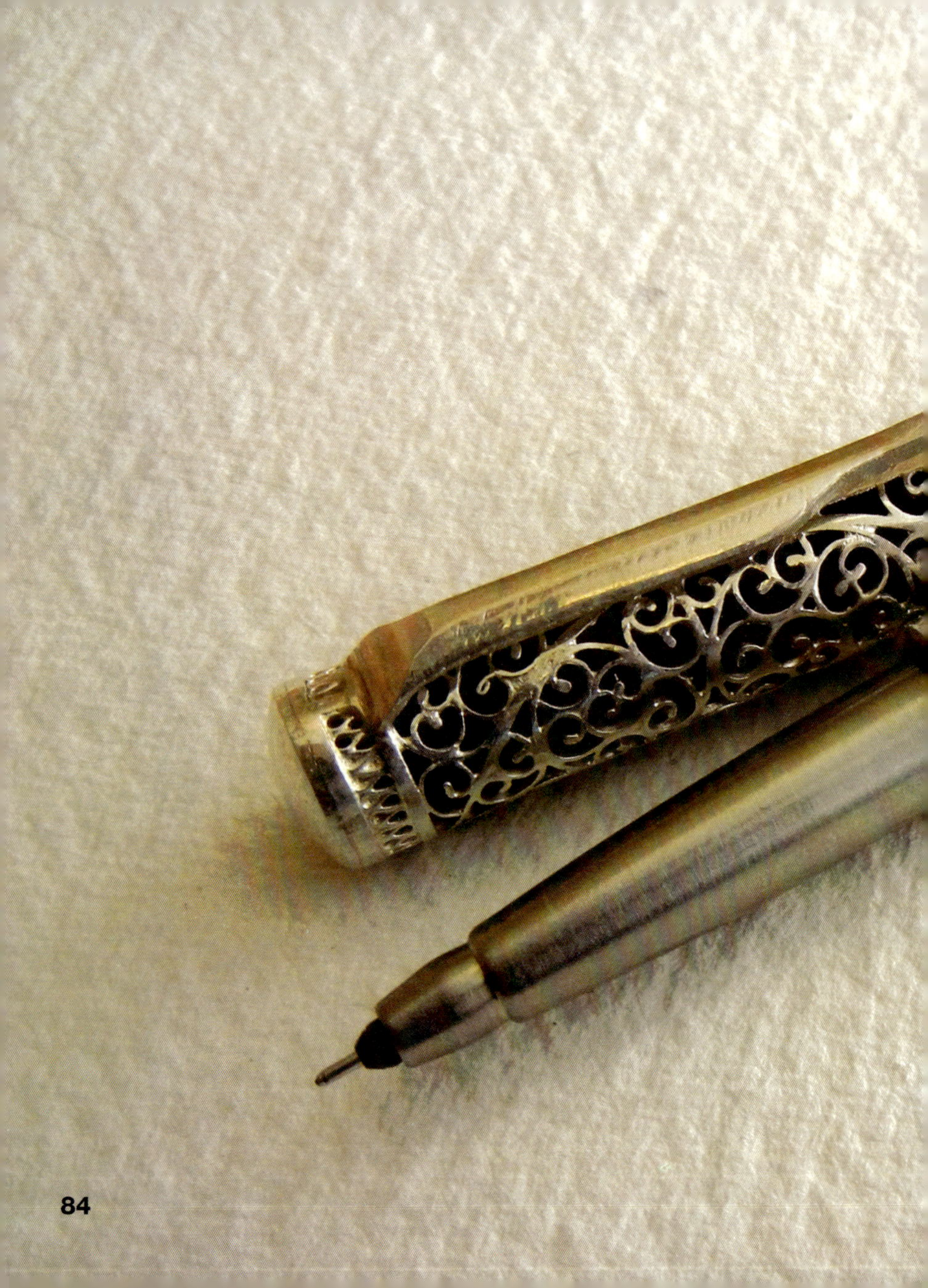

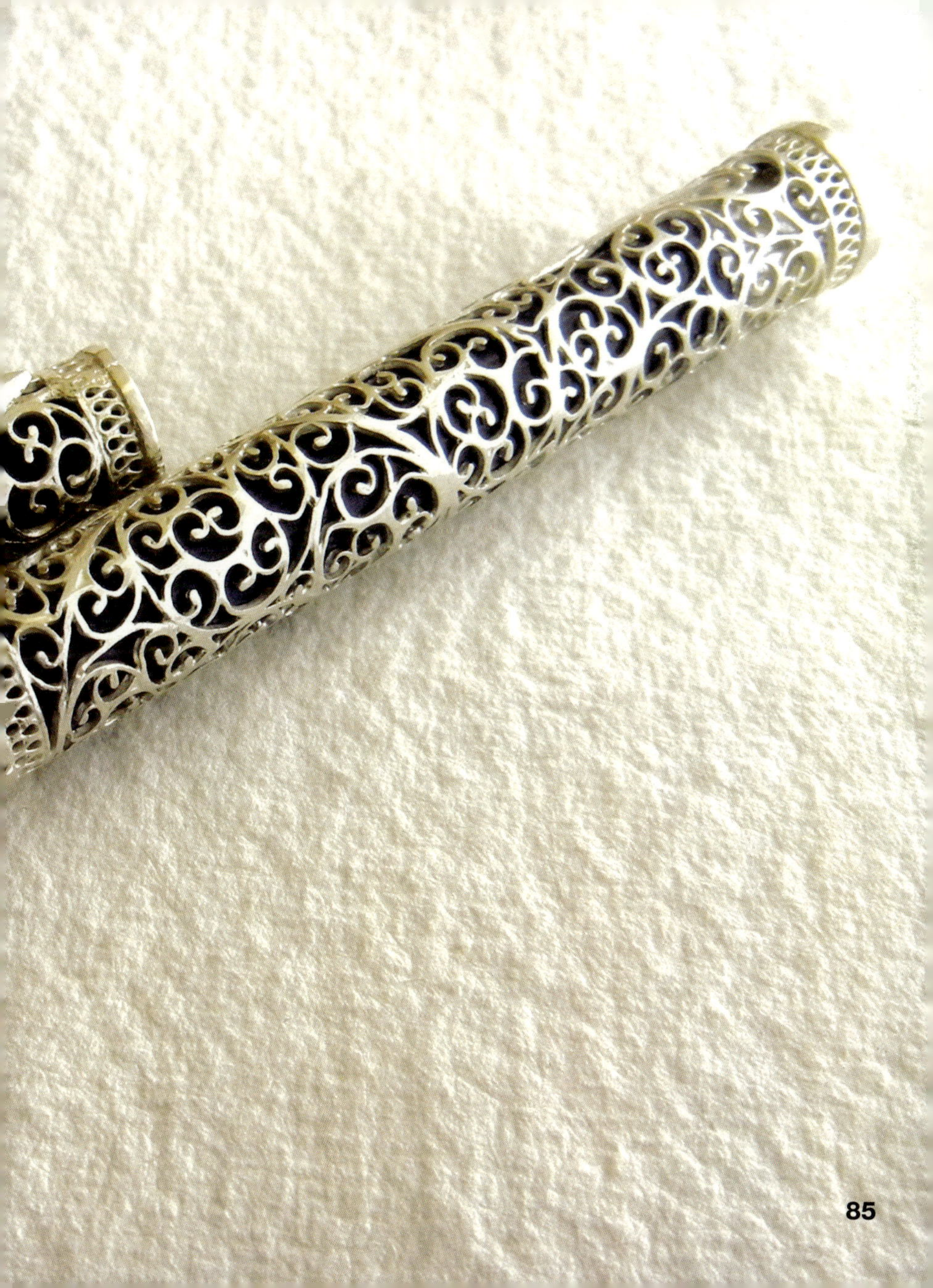

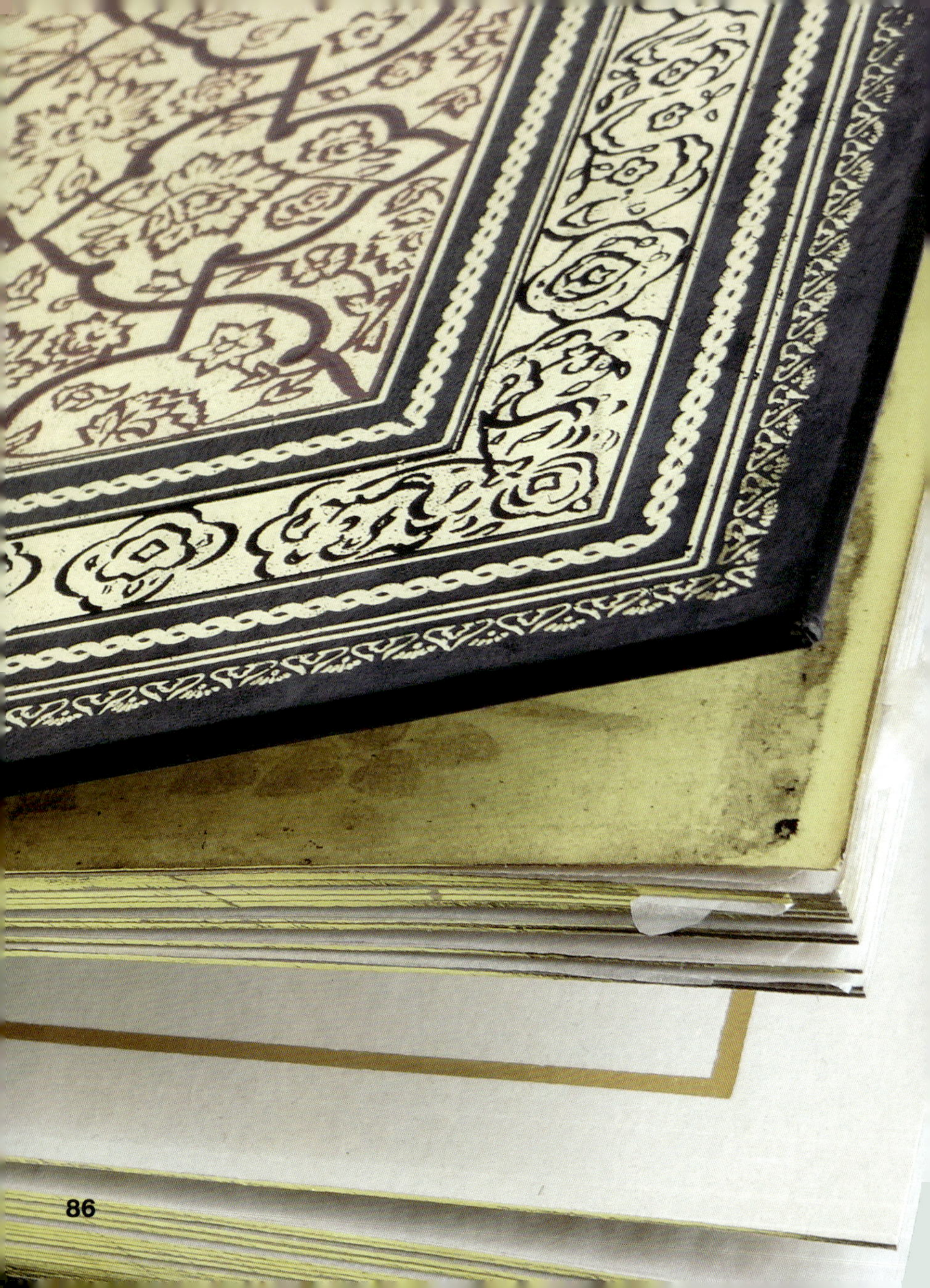

No machine can compare with a man's hands. Machinery gives speed, power, complete uniformity, and precision, but it cannot give creativity, adaptability, freedom, heterogeneity. These the machine is incapable of, hence the superiority of the hand, which no amount of rationalism can negate. Man prefers the creative and the free to the fixed and the standardized.

~ Soetsu Yanagi
The Unknown Craftsman

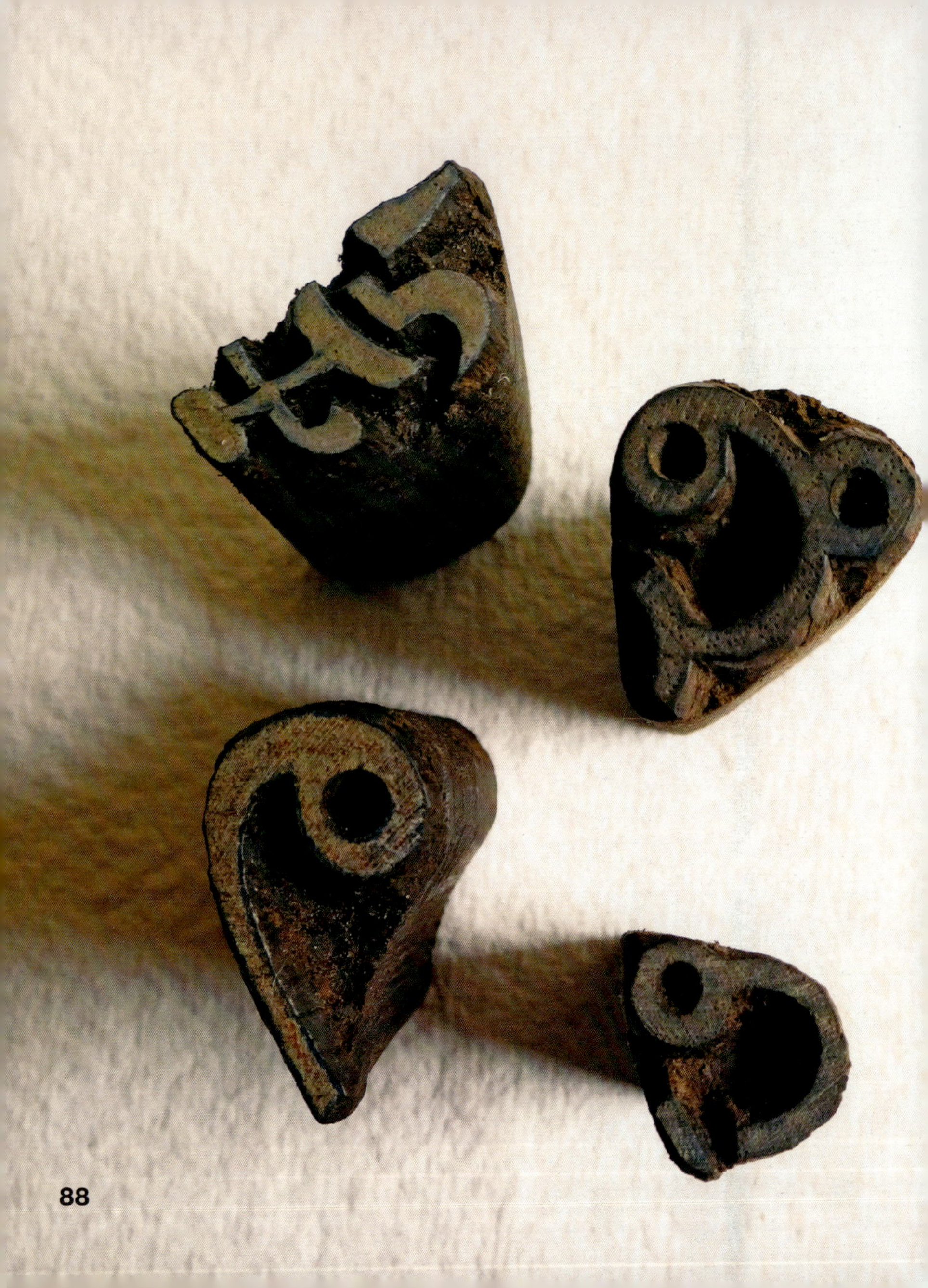

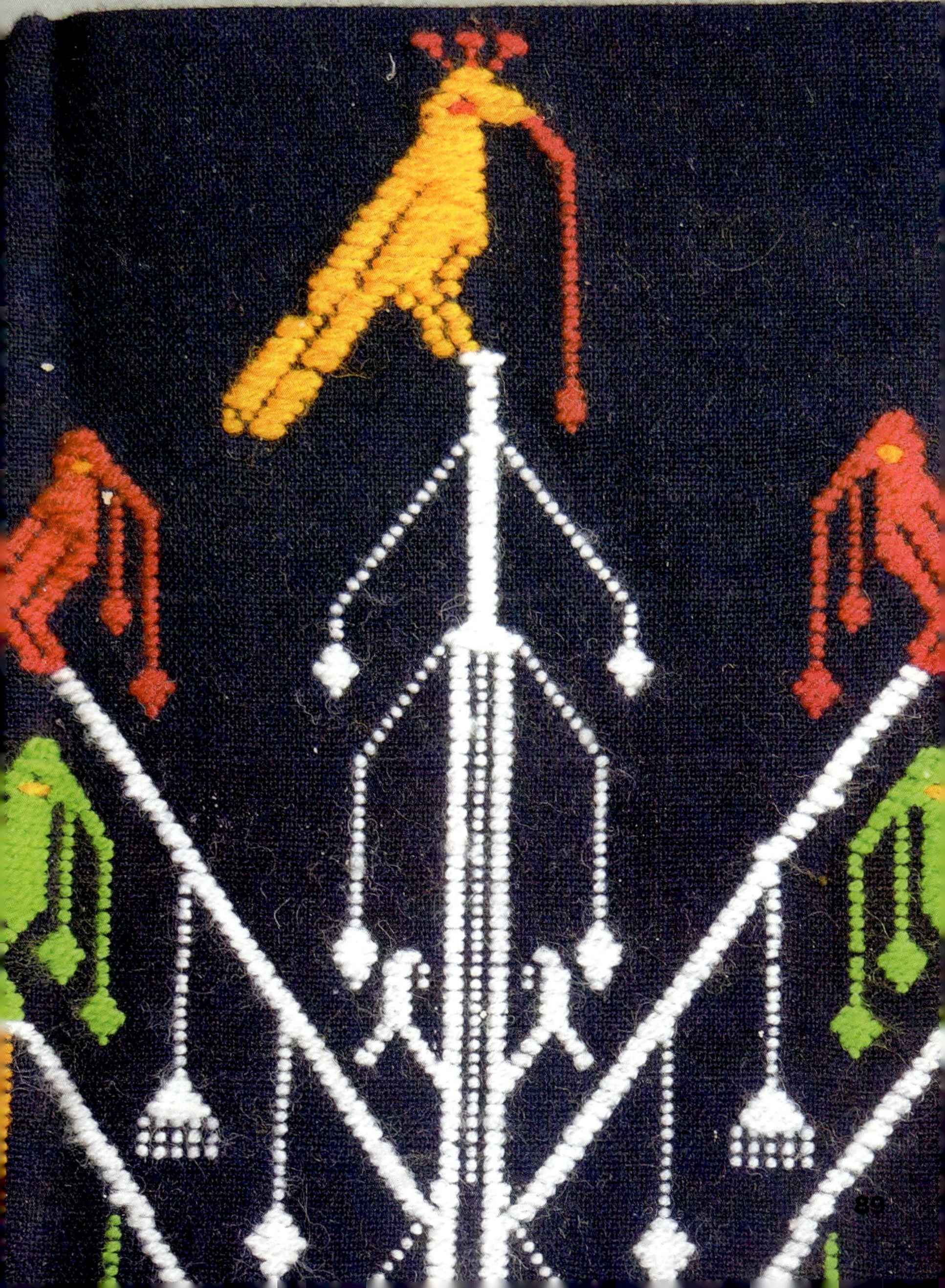

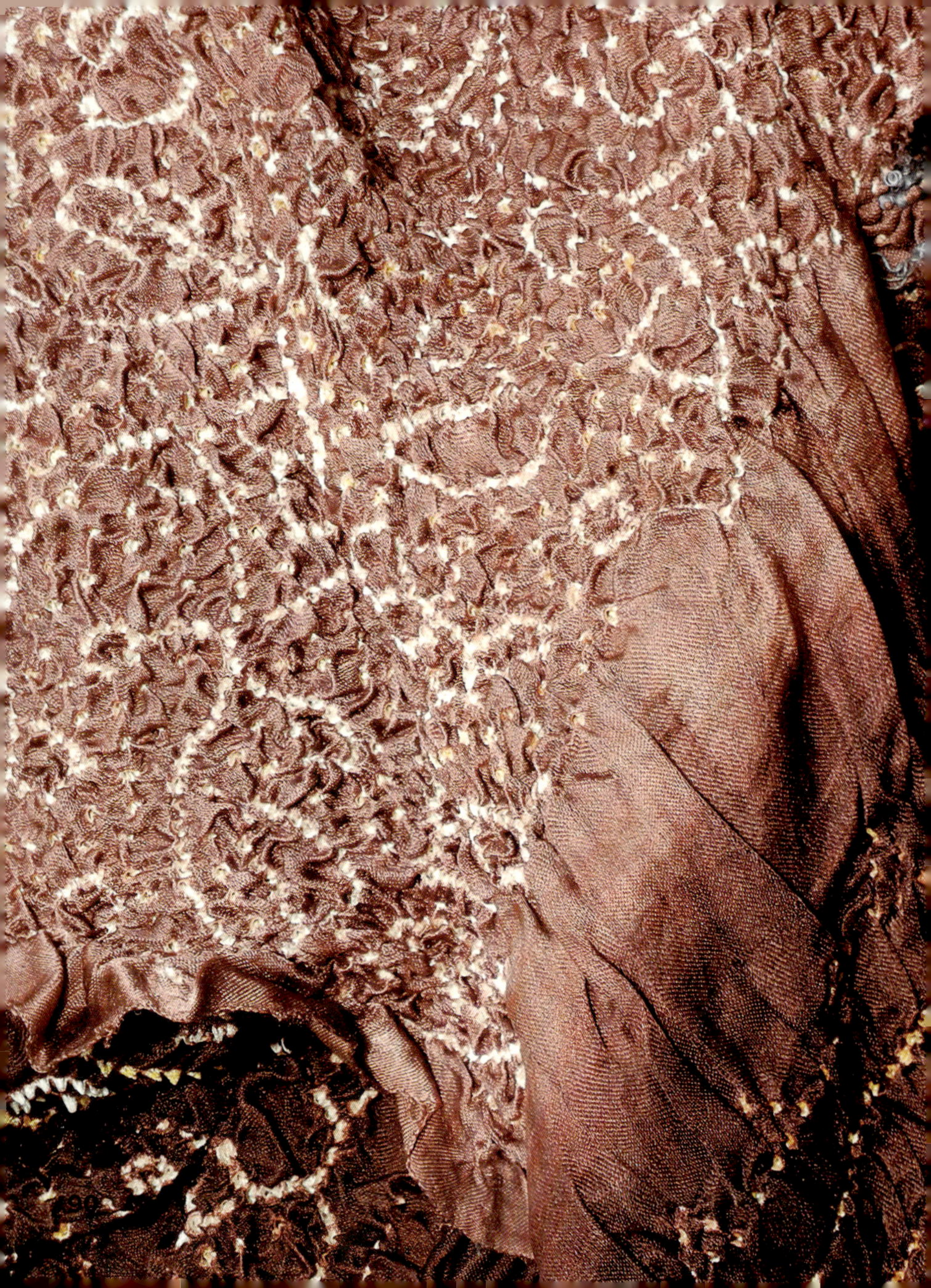

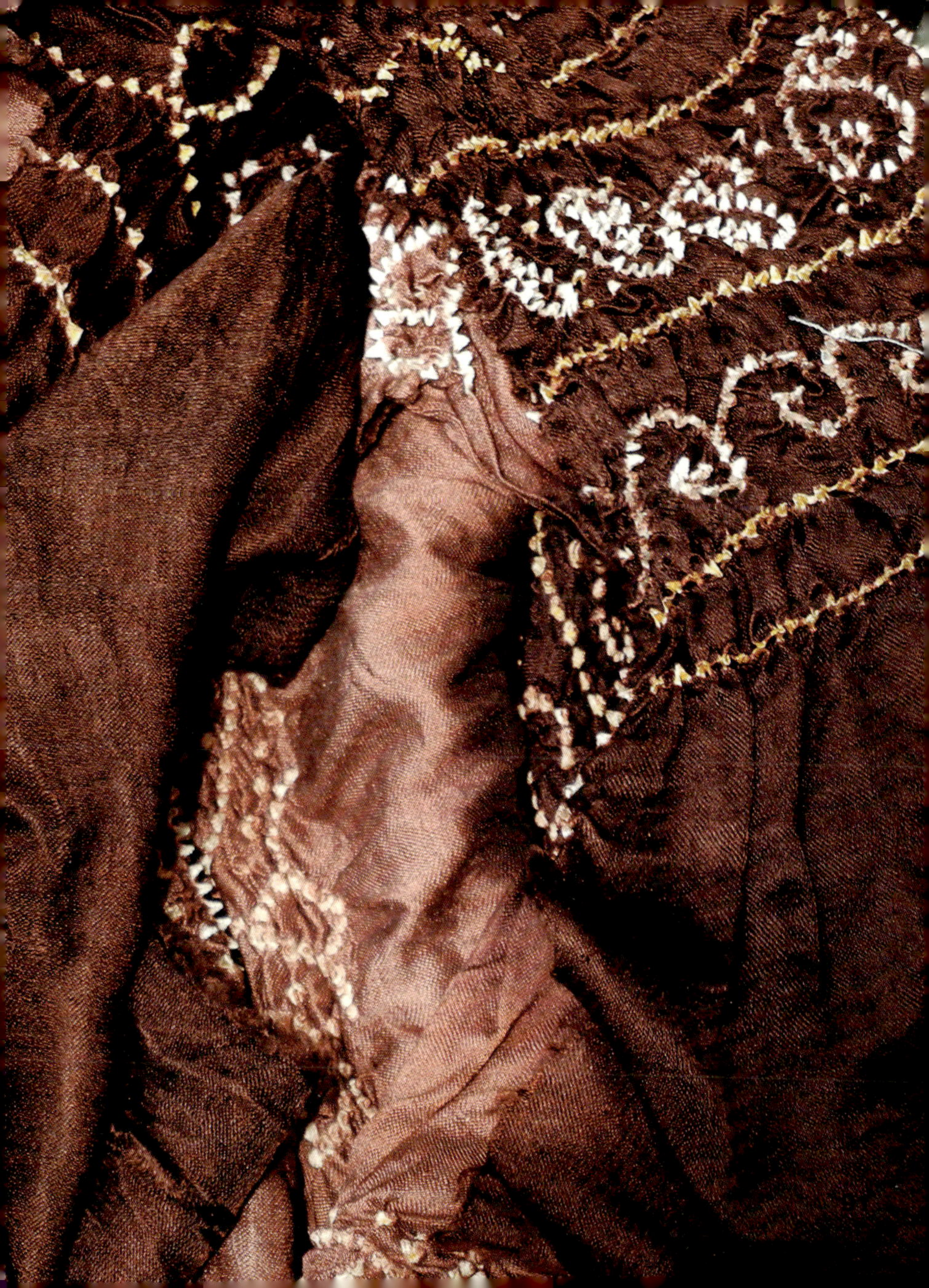

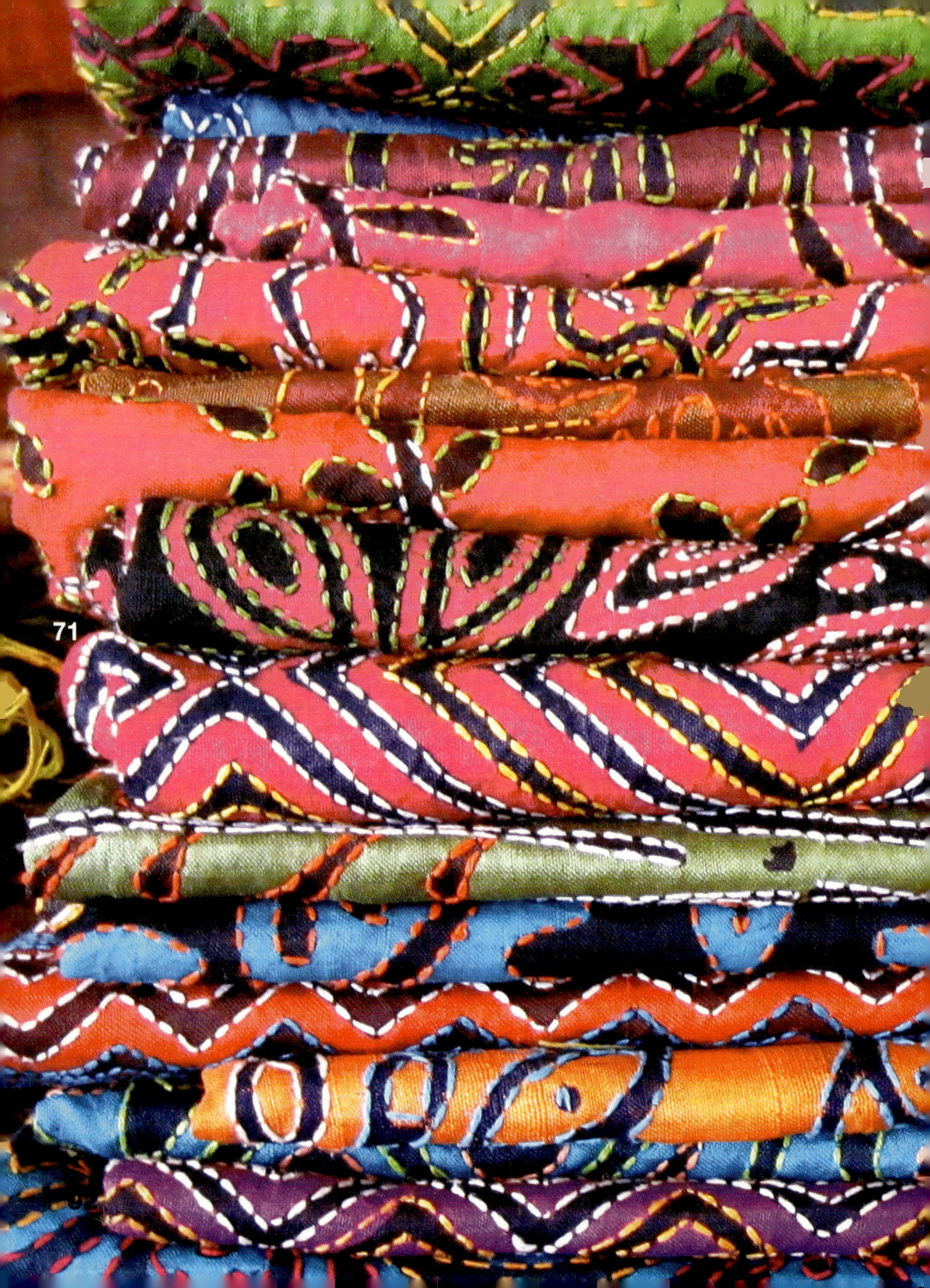

71

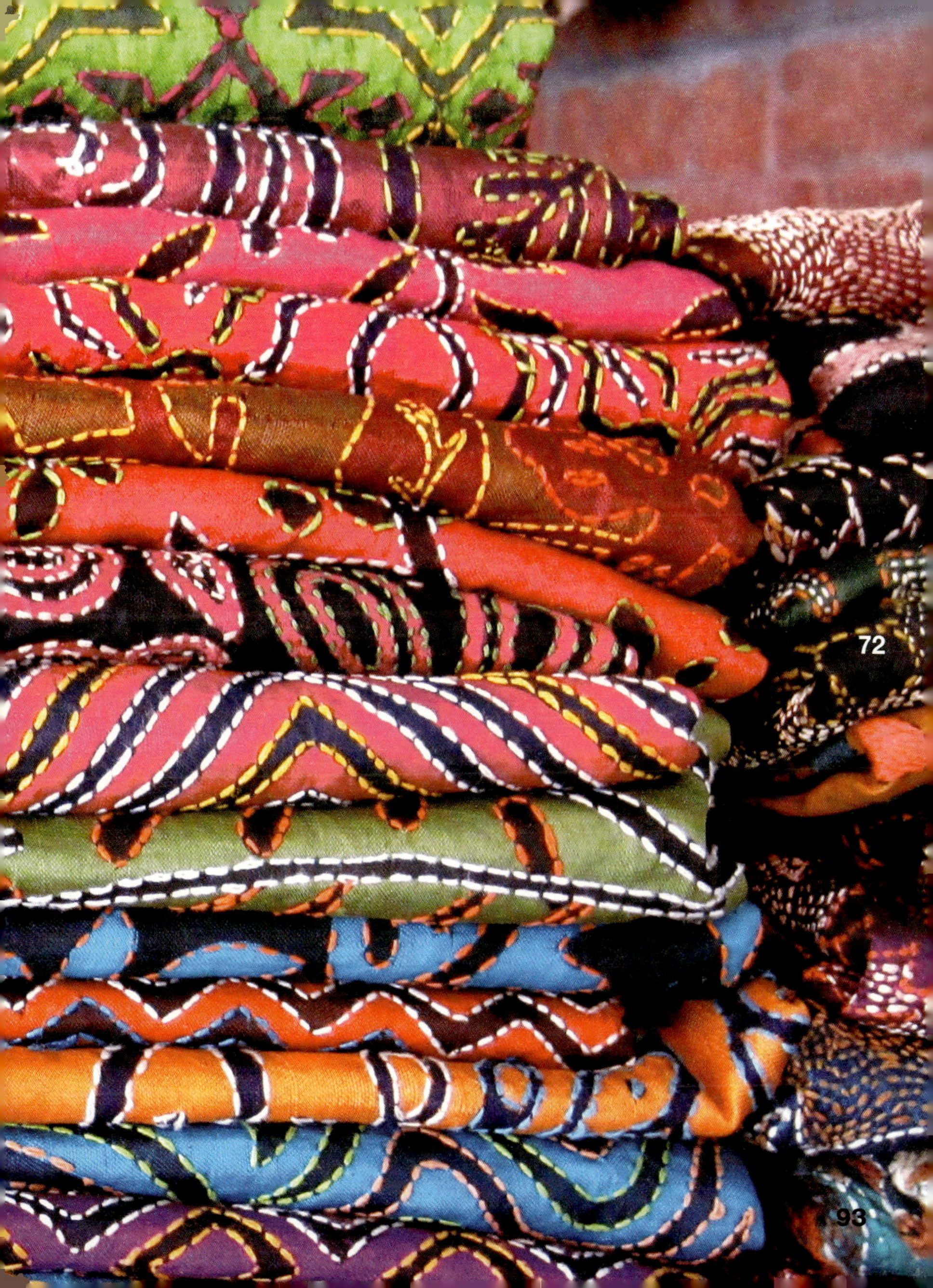
72

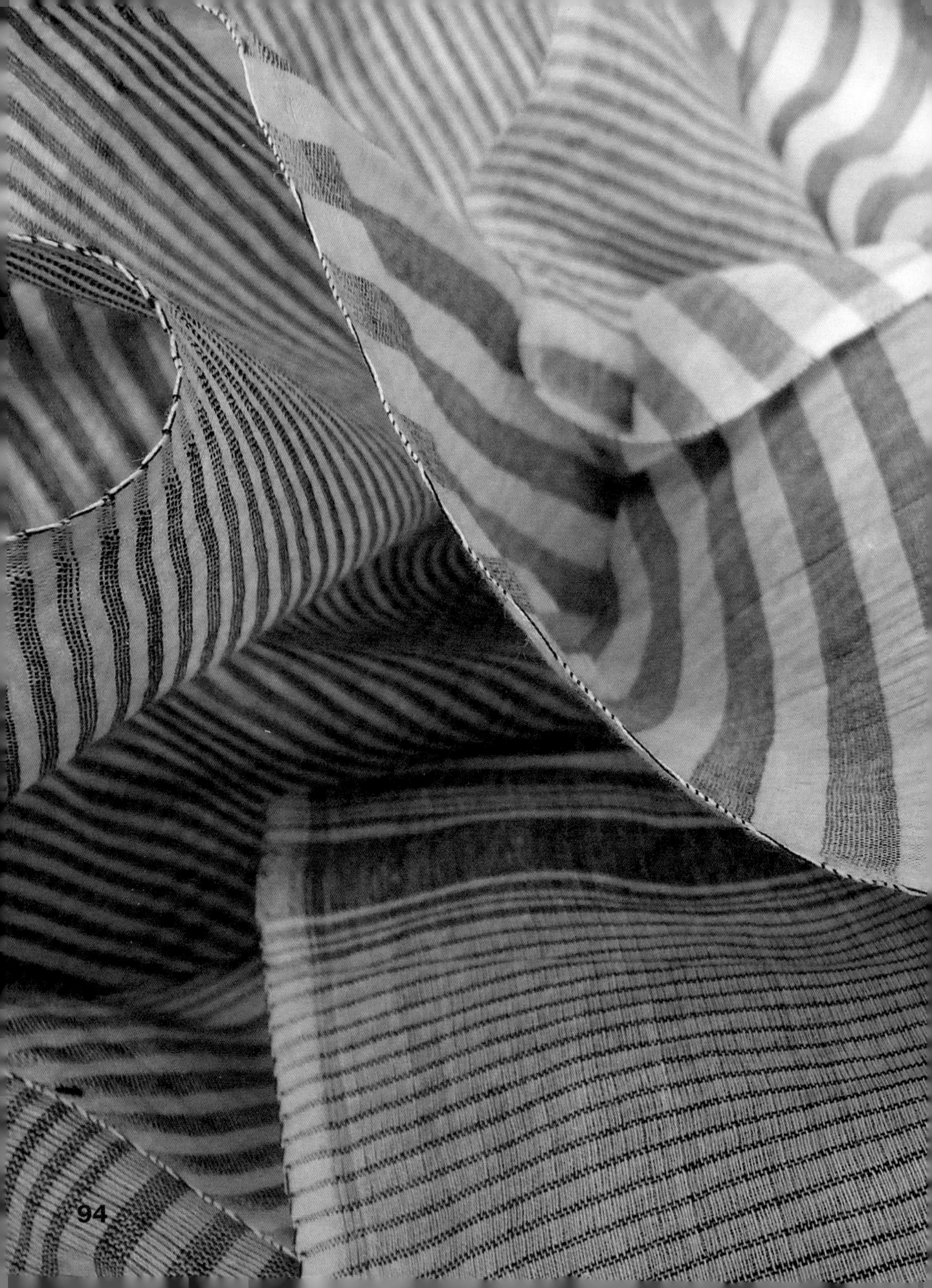

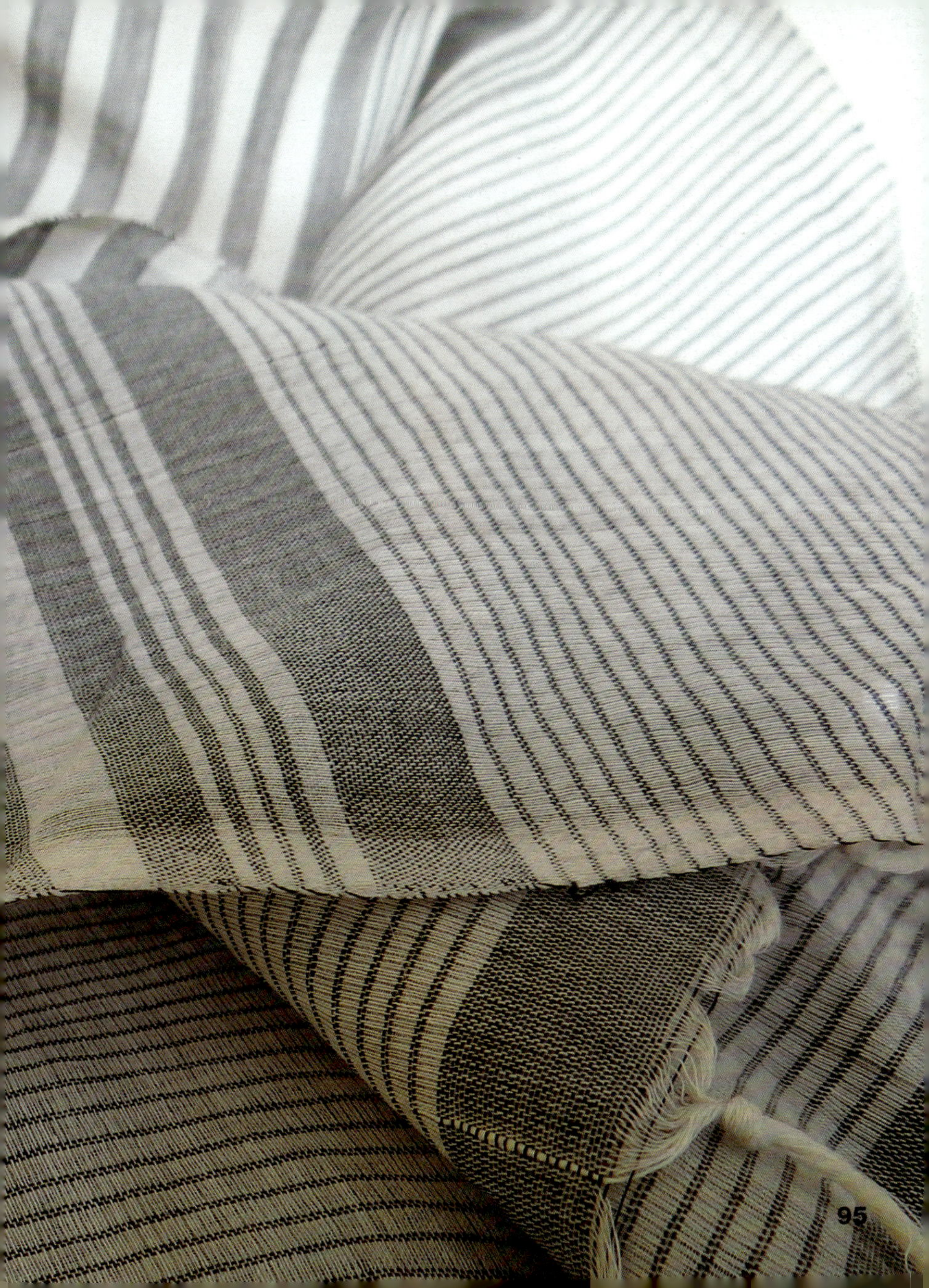

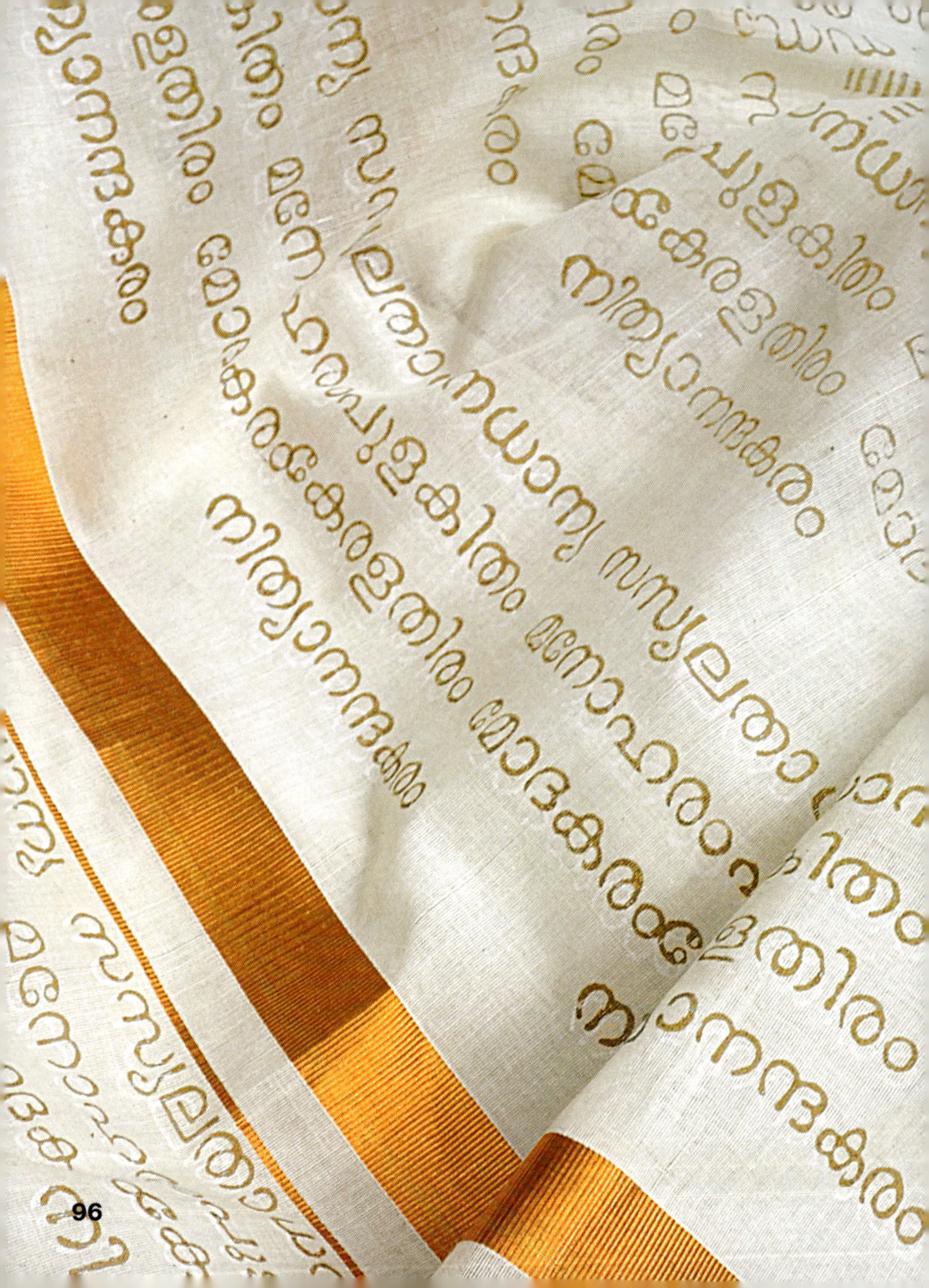

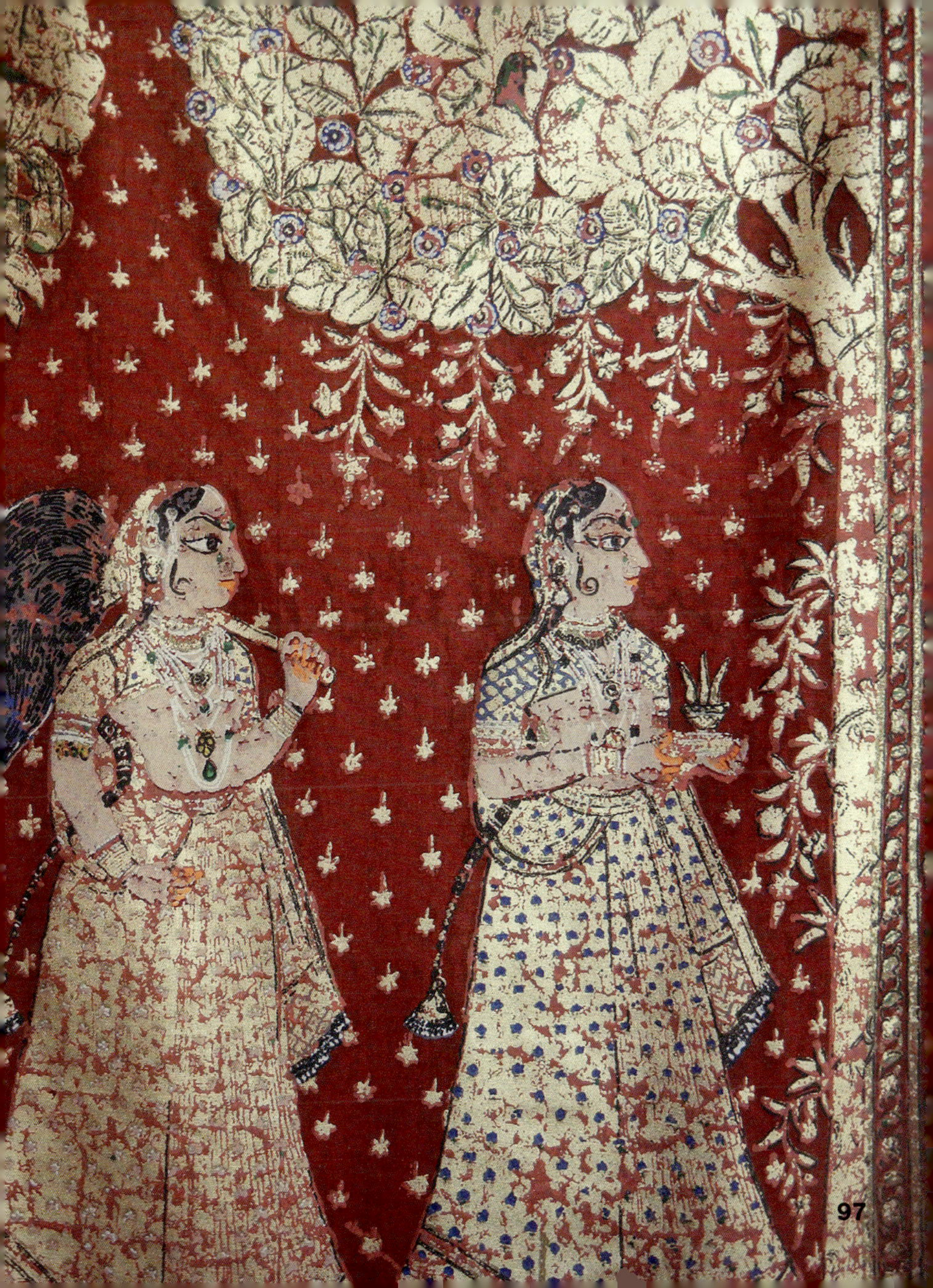

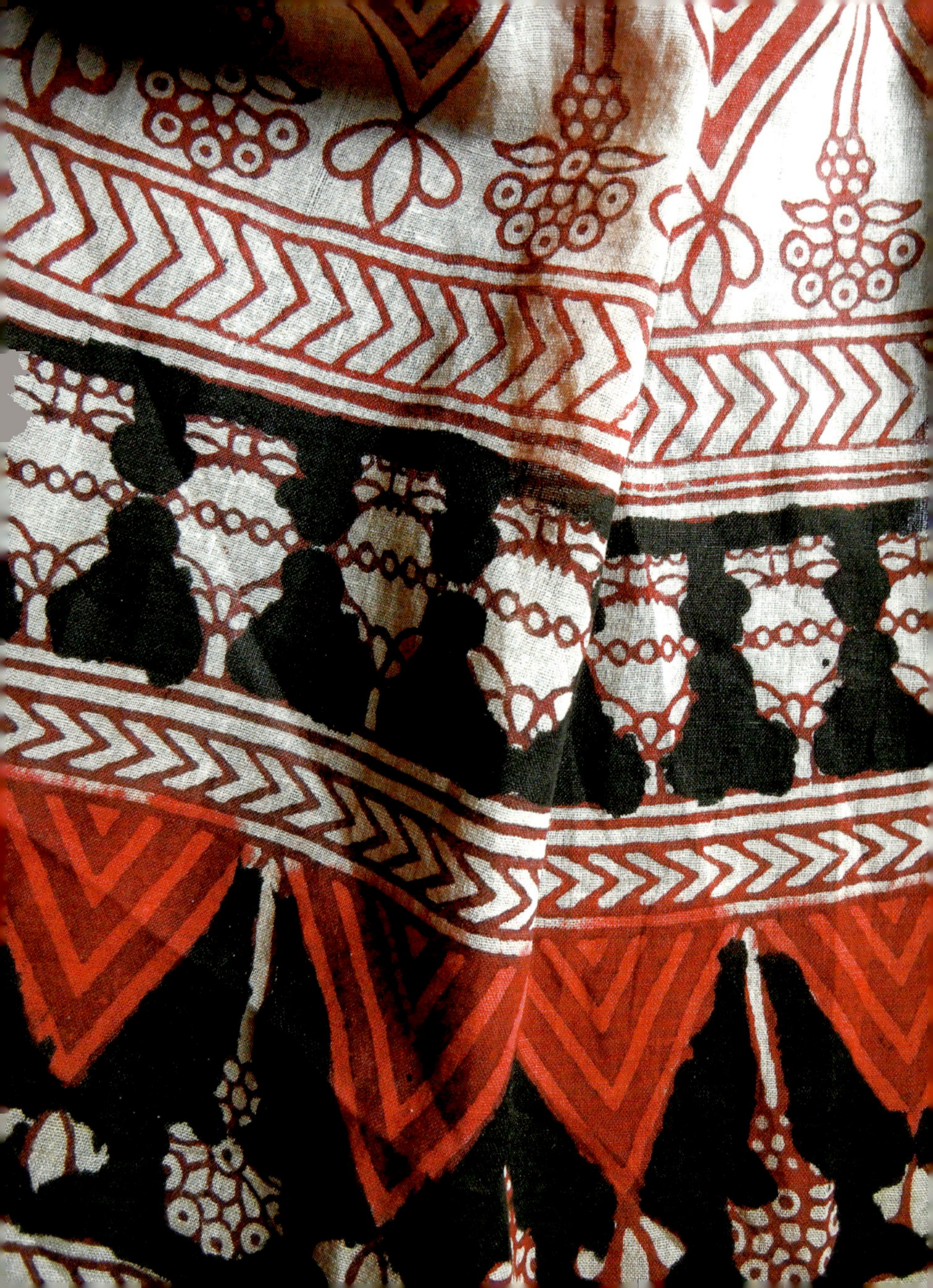

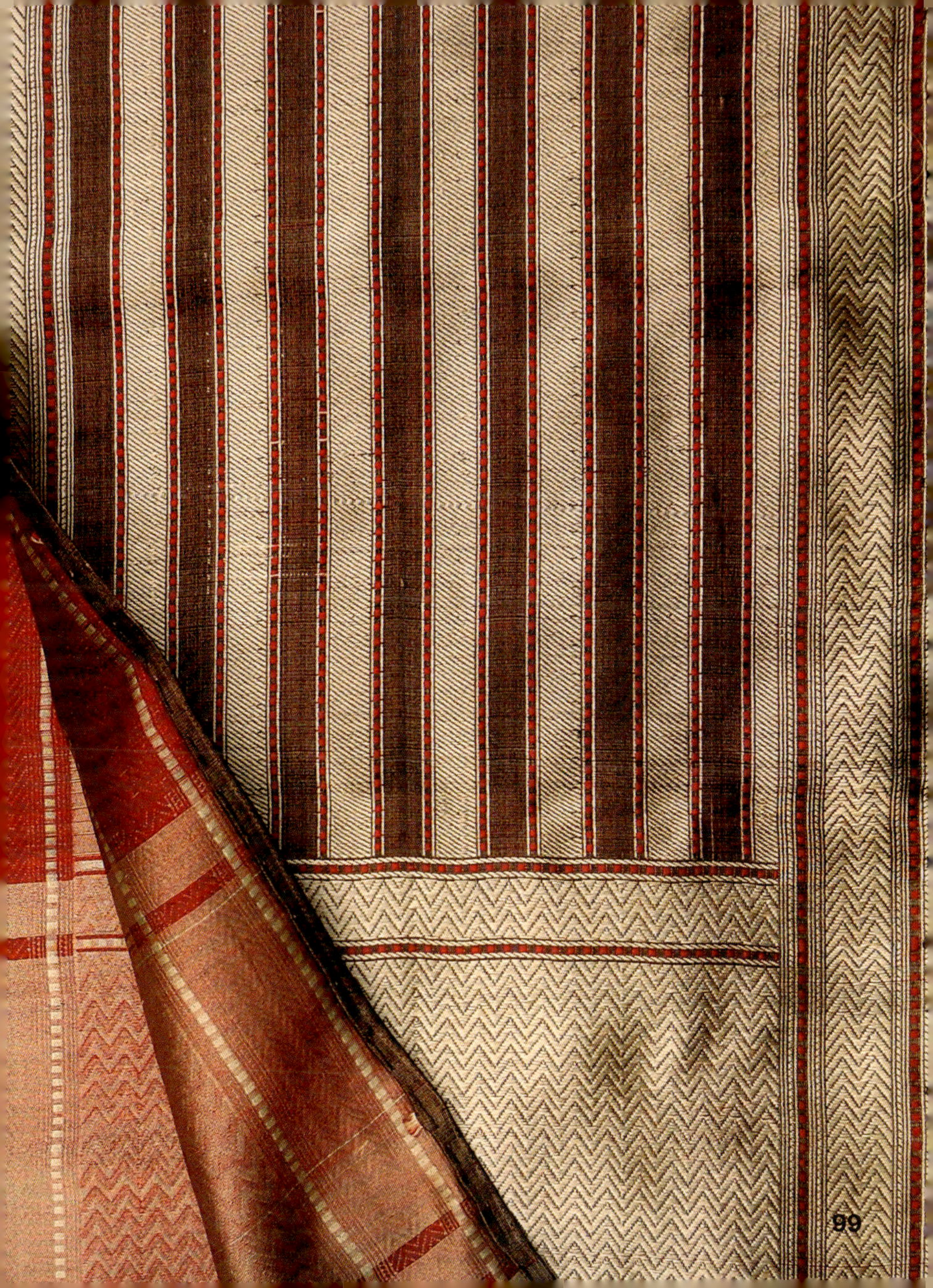

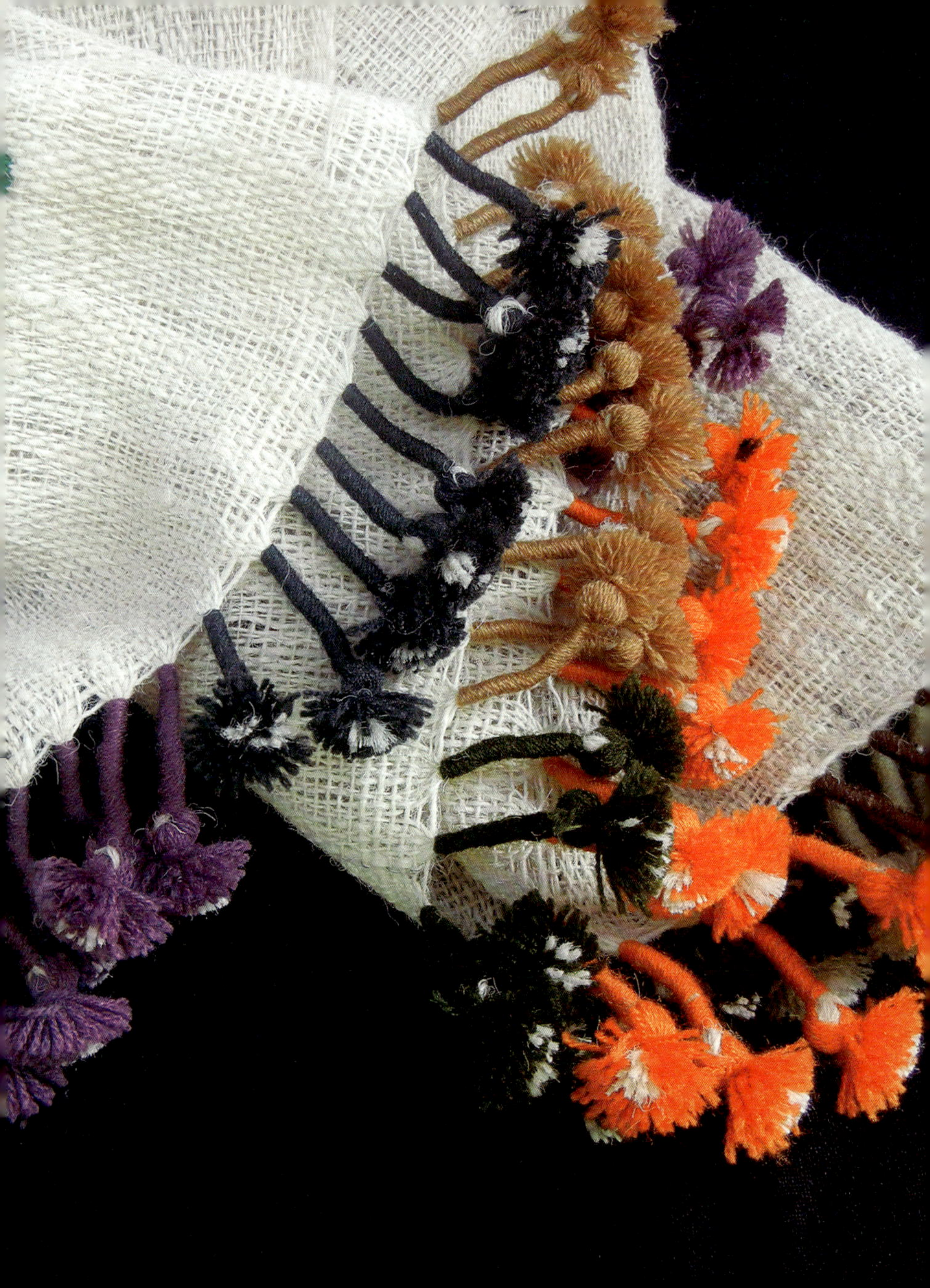

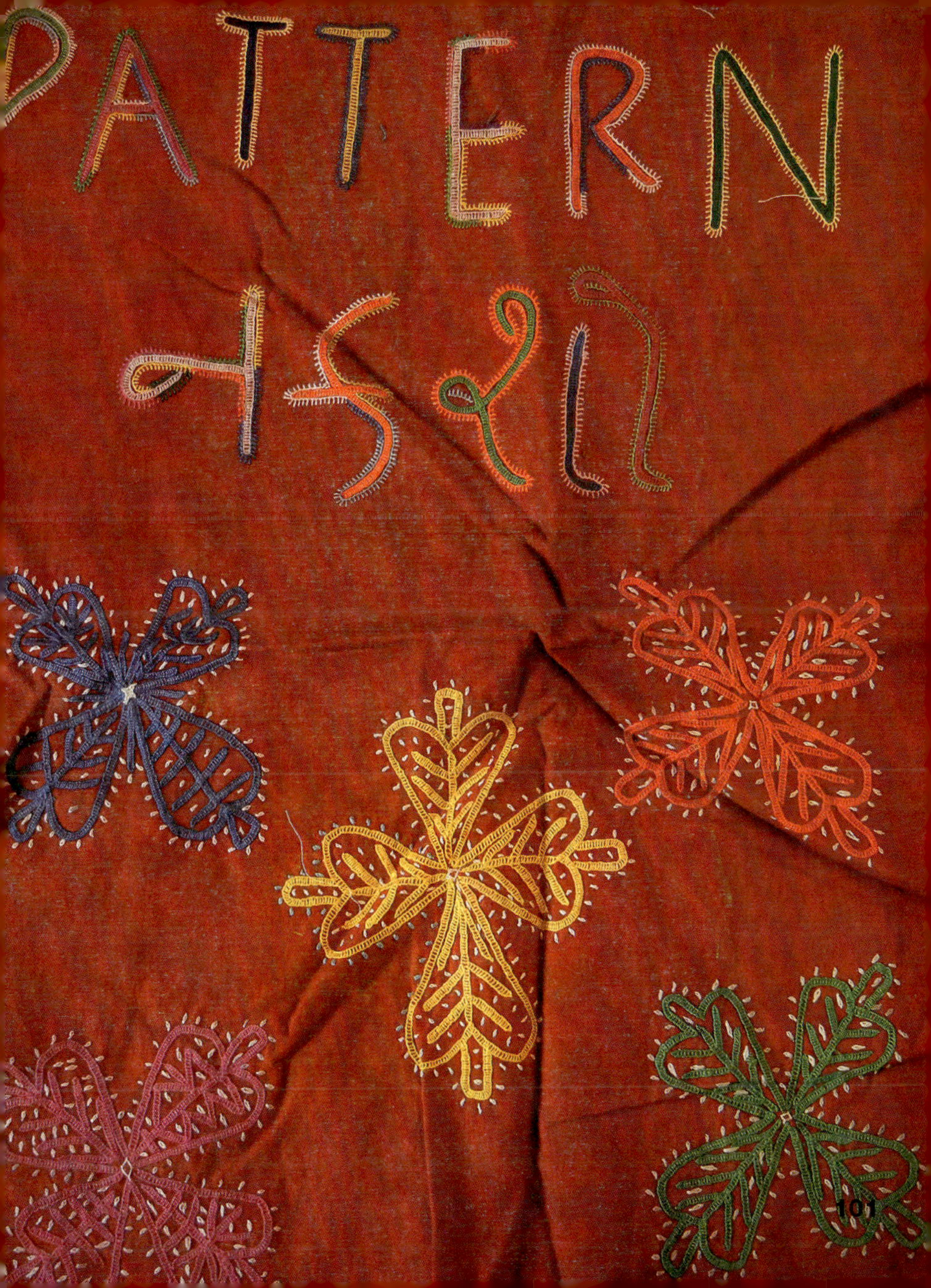
PATTERN
નકશી

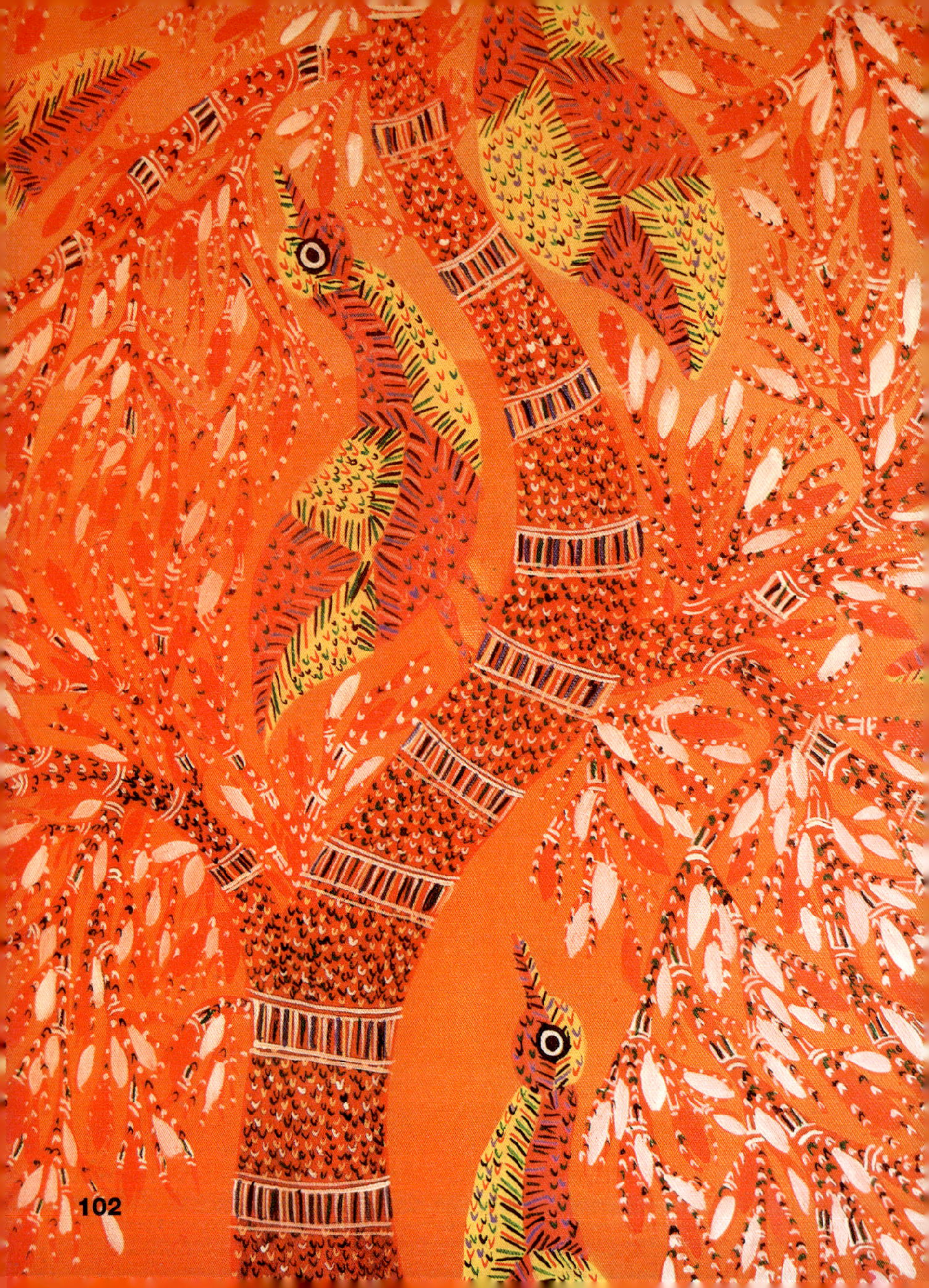

The important part which craftsmen, more especially oriental craftsmen, have always played in the world's history as missionaries of civilization, culture, and religion, is not generally realized by bookmen. Even at the present day the Indian craftsman, deeply versed in his Silpa Sastras , learned in folk-lore and in national epic literature, is, though excluded from Indian universities – or, rather, on that account – far more highly cultured, intellectually and spiritually, than the average Indian graduate. In medieval times the craftsman's intellectual influence, being creative and not merely assimilative, was at least as great as that of the priest and bookman.

~ E.B. Havell
Indian Sculpture and Painting

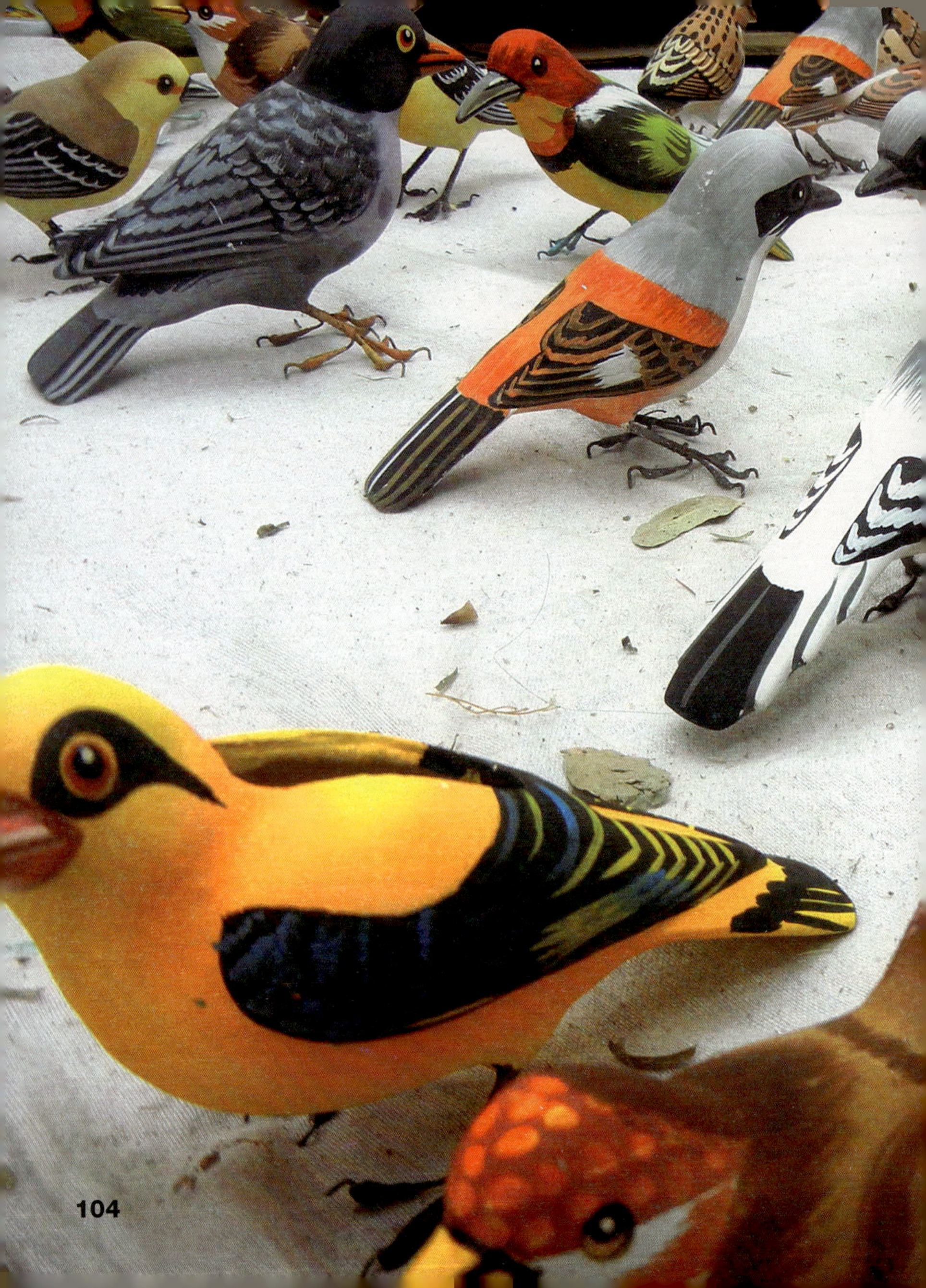

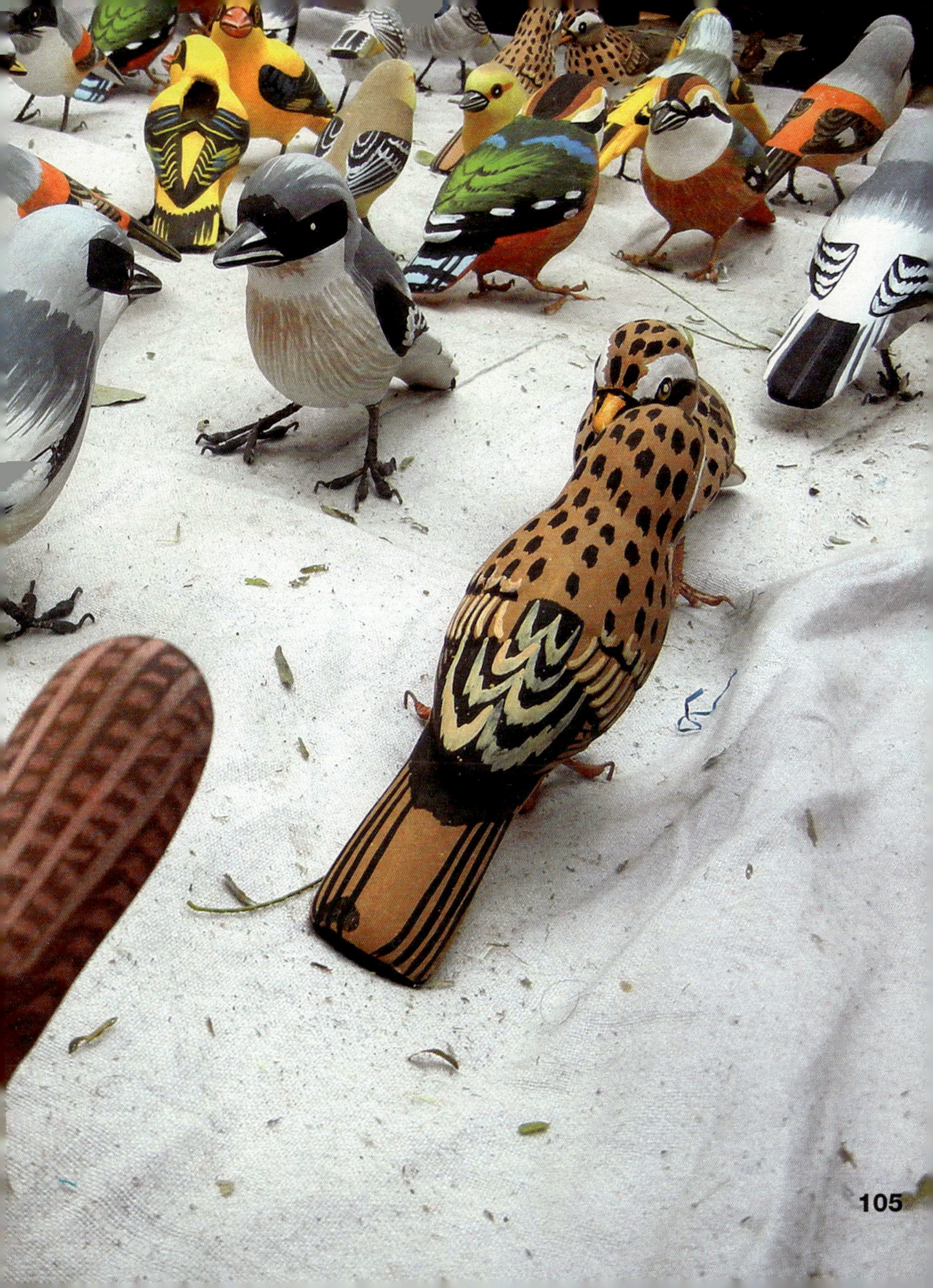

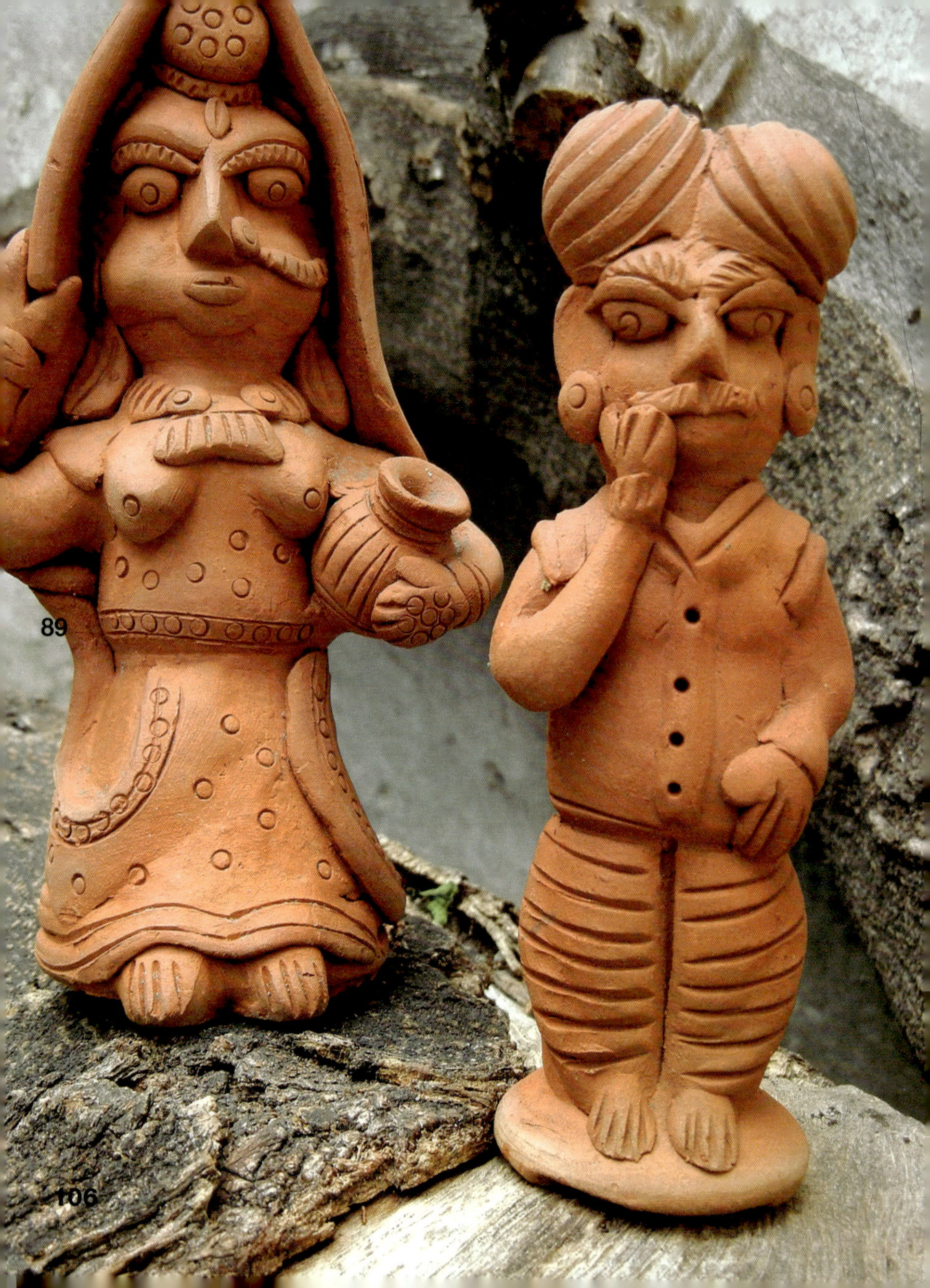

89

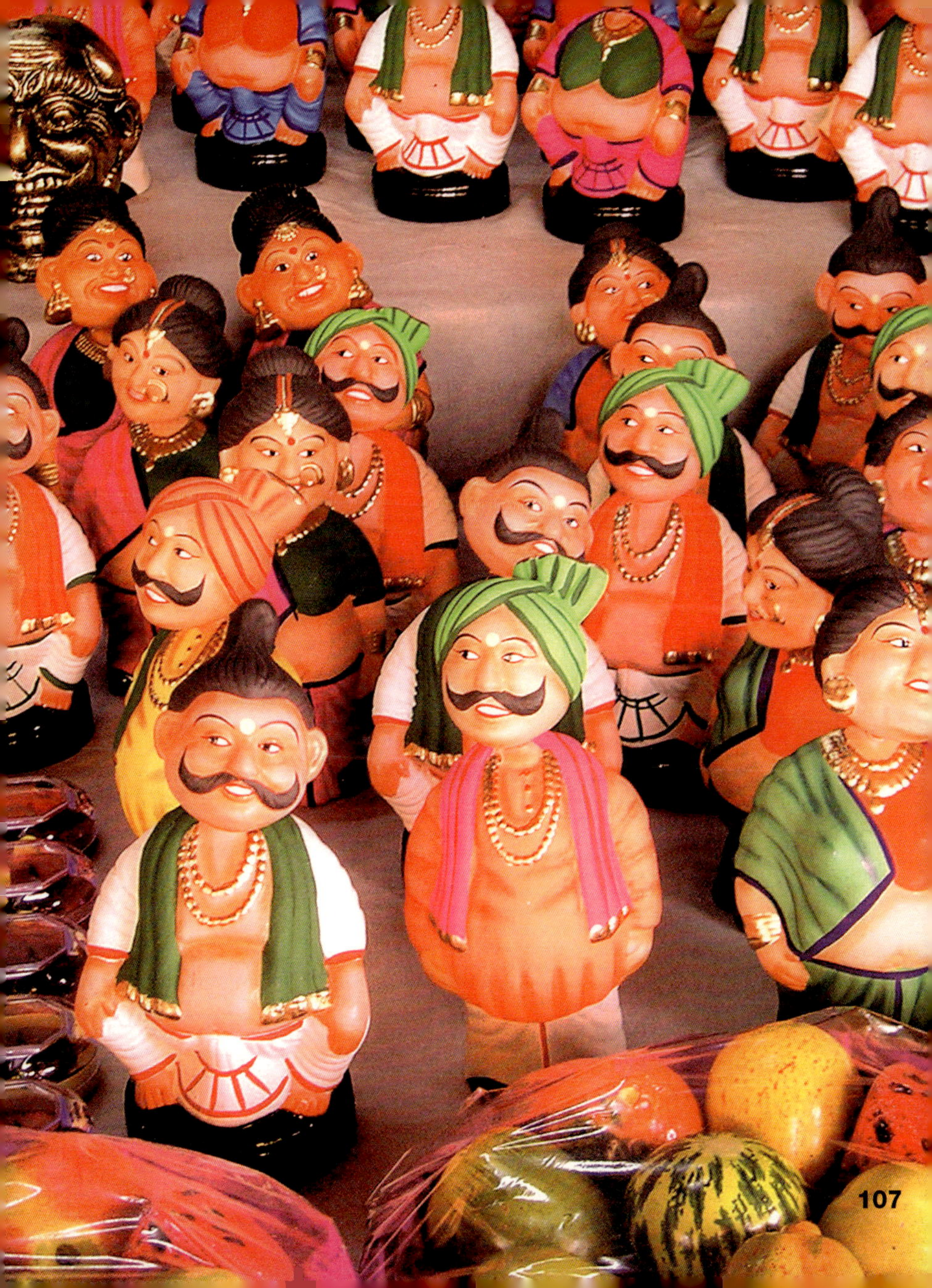

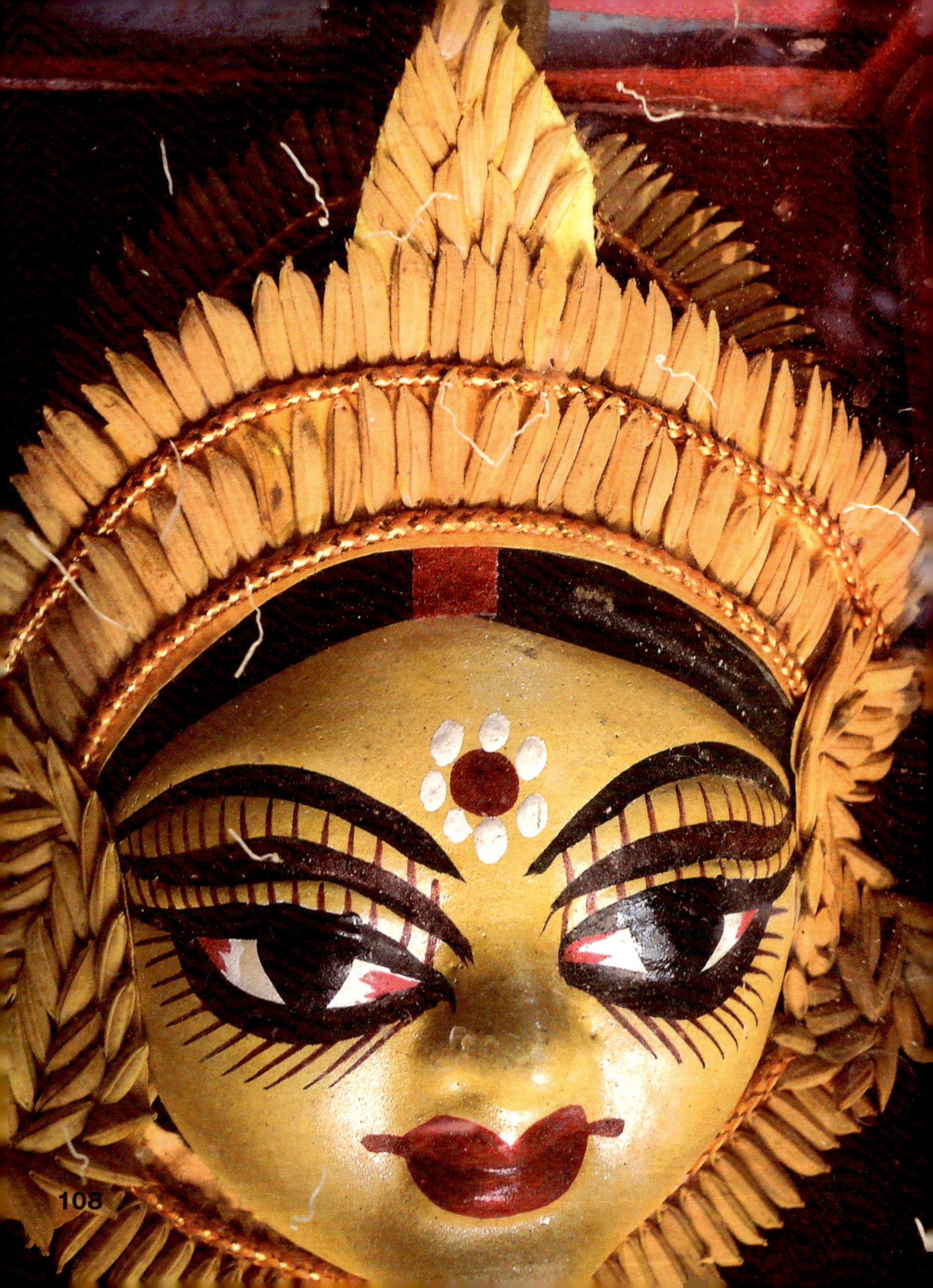

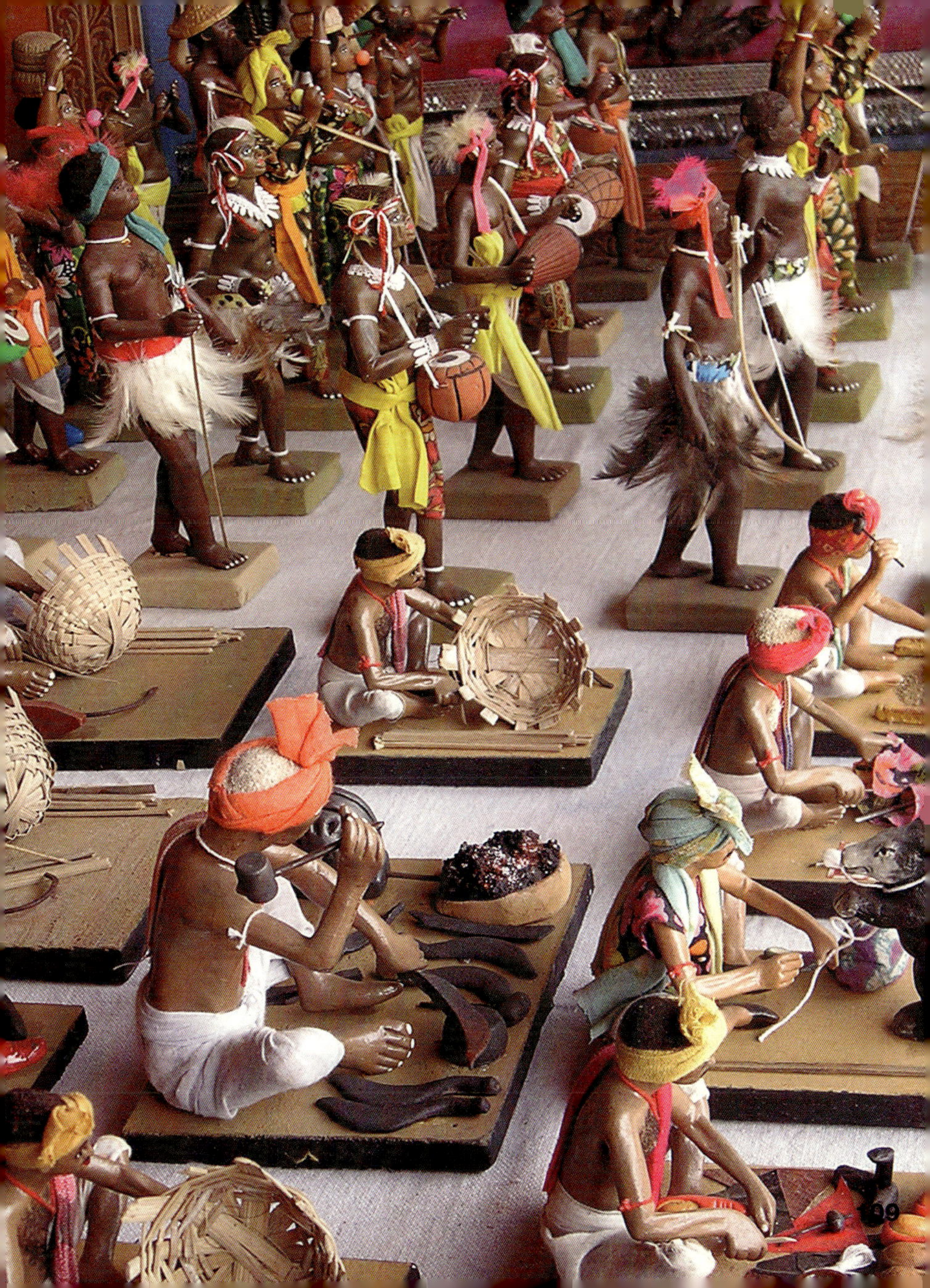

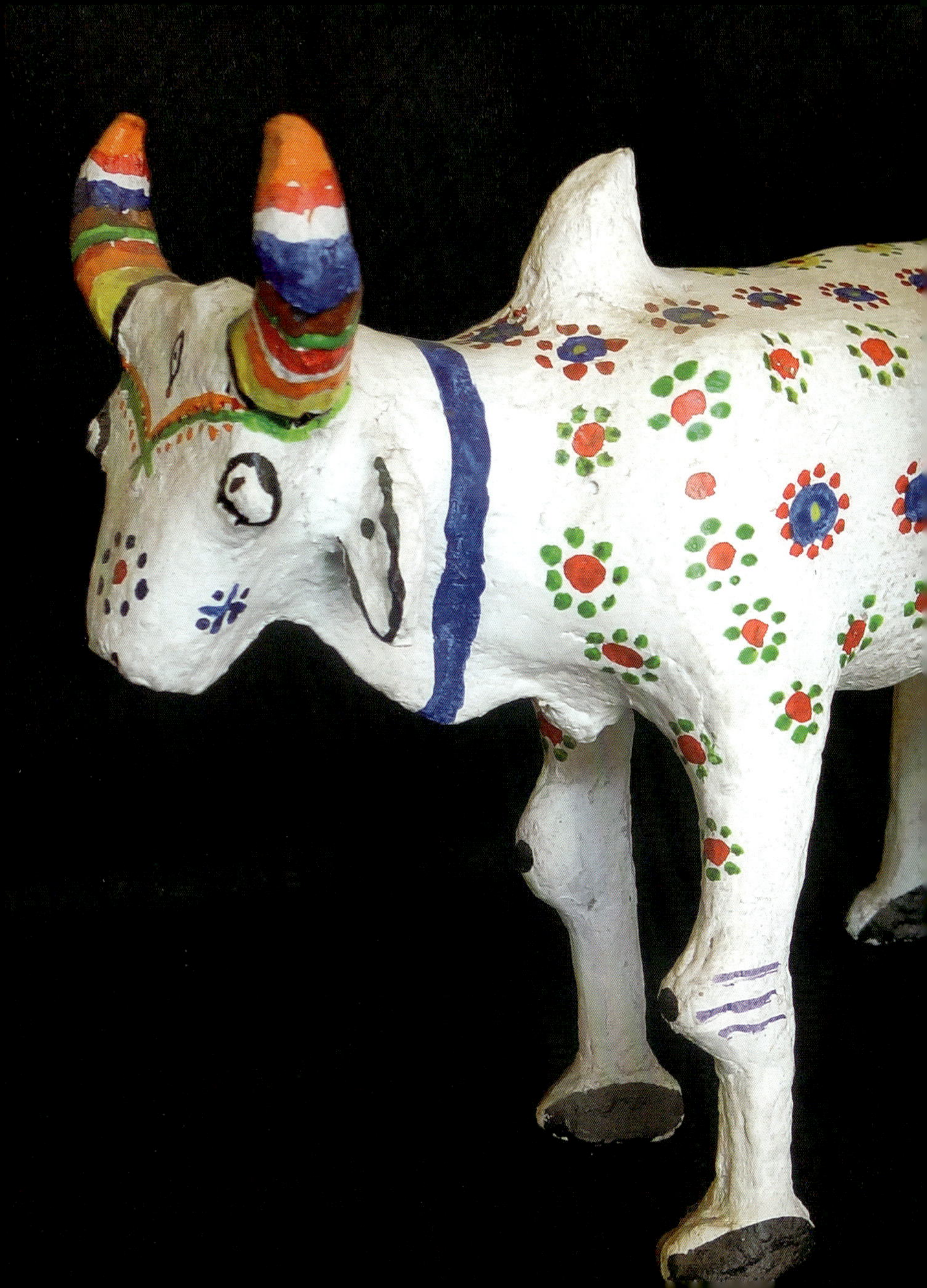

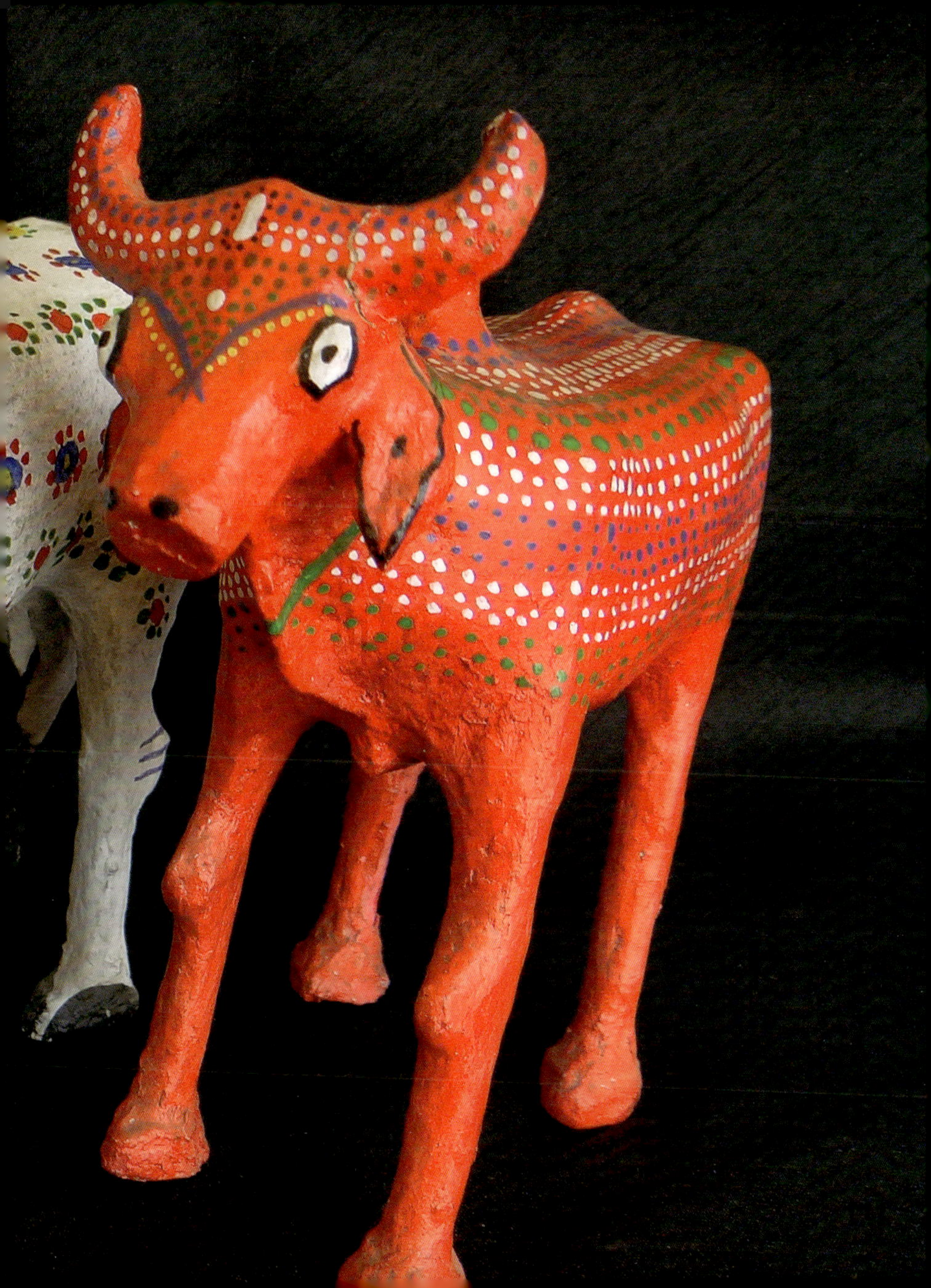

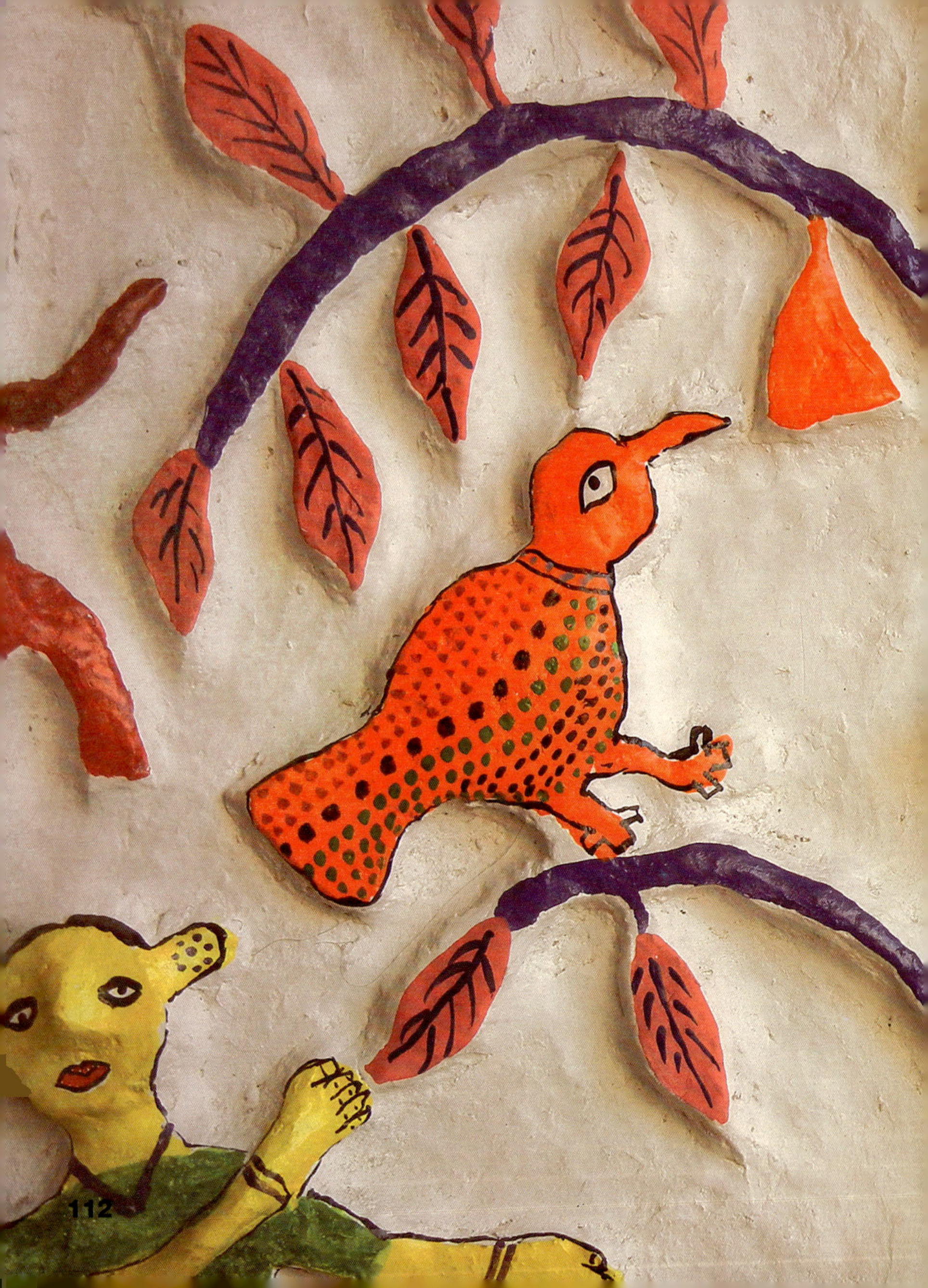

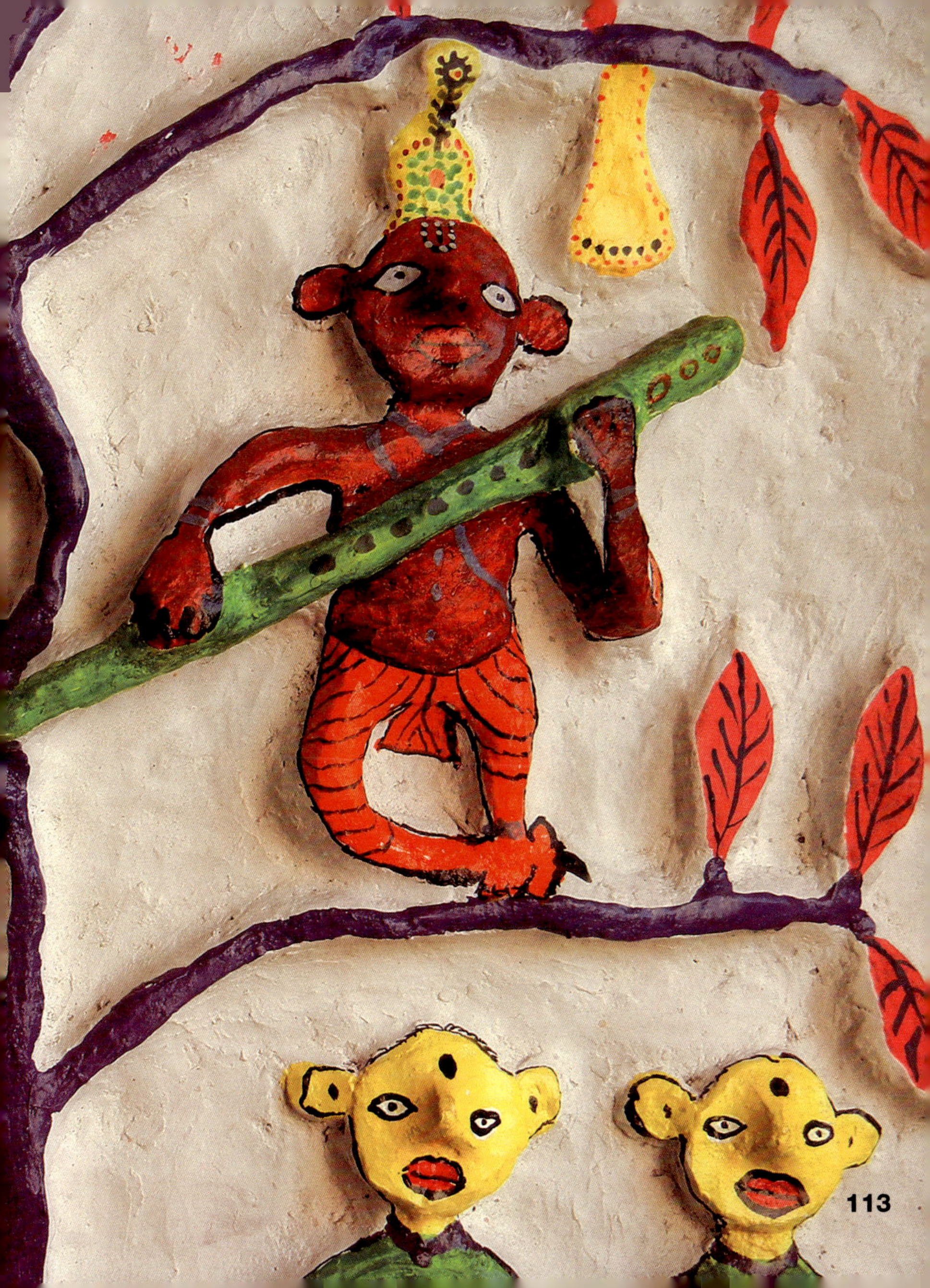

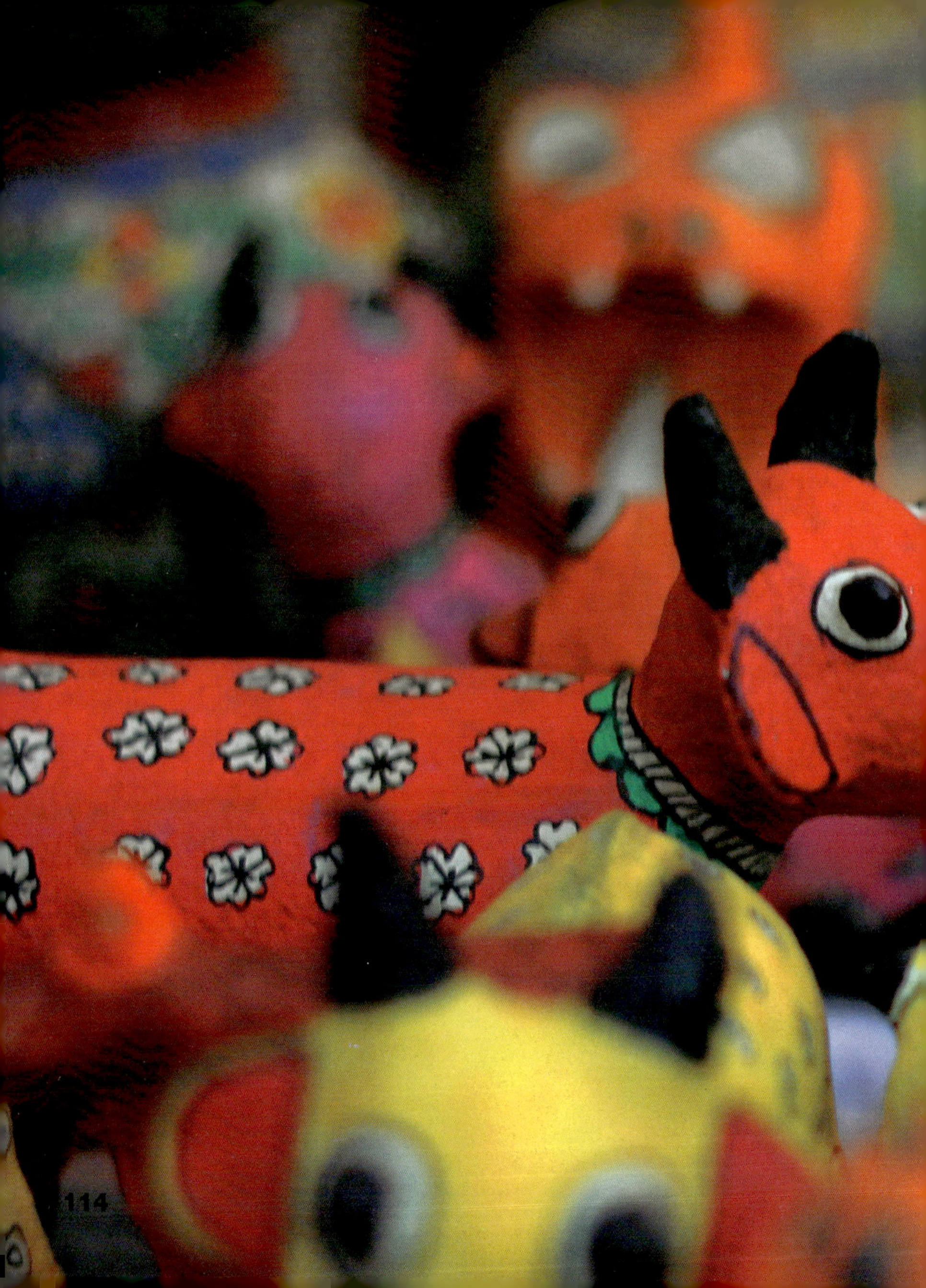

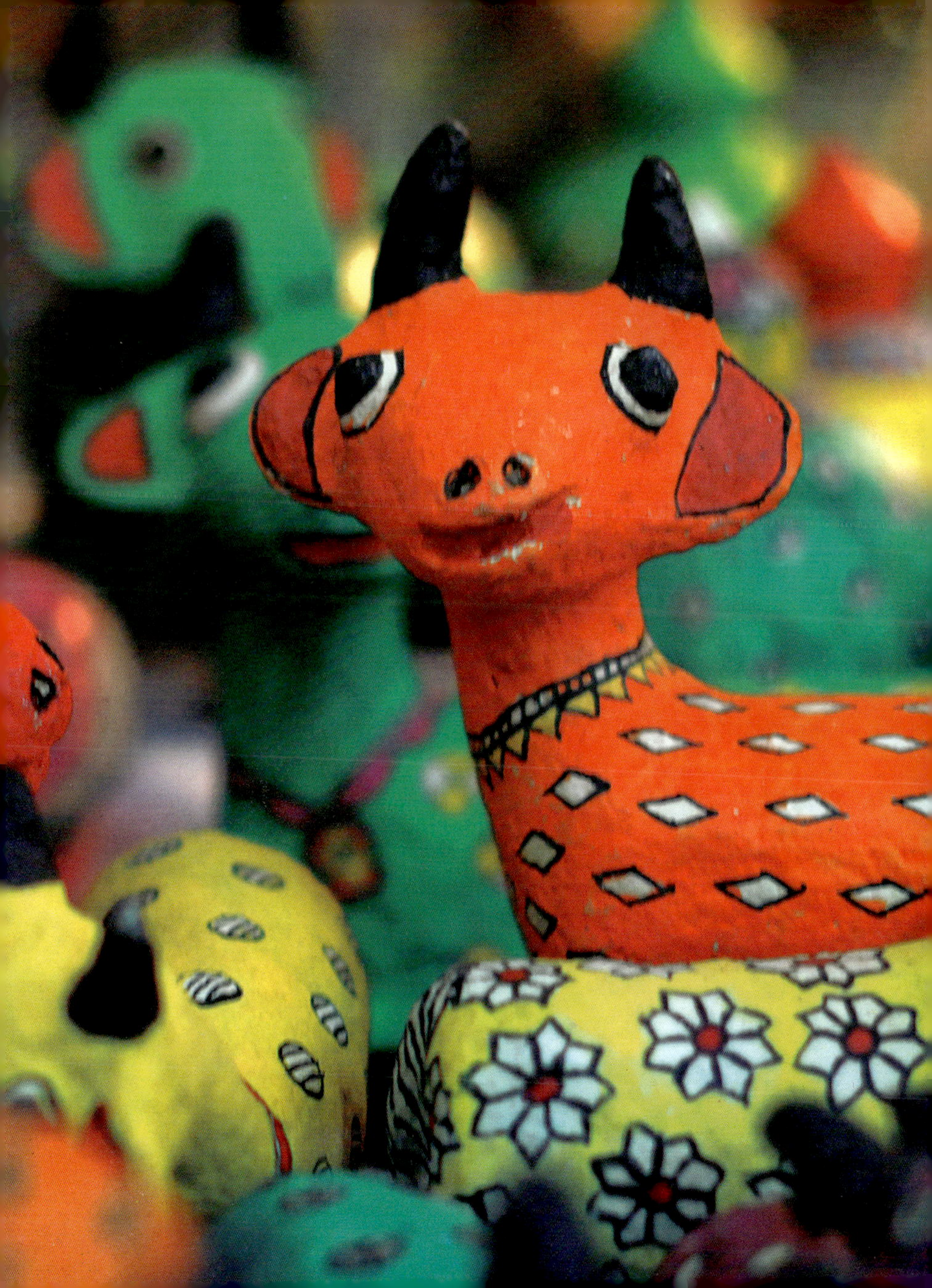

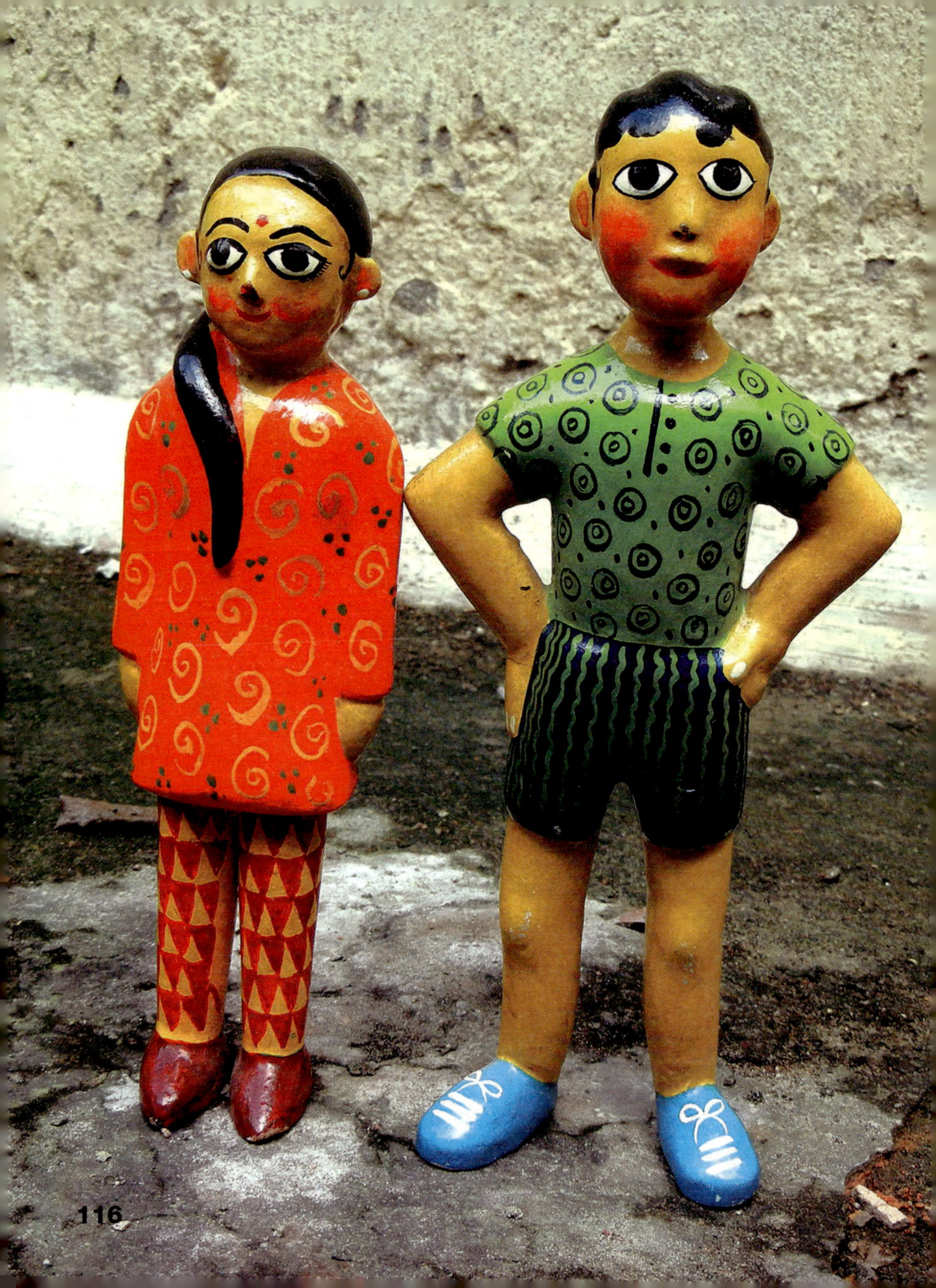

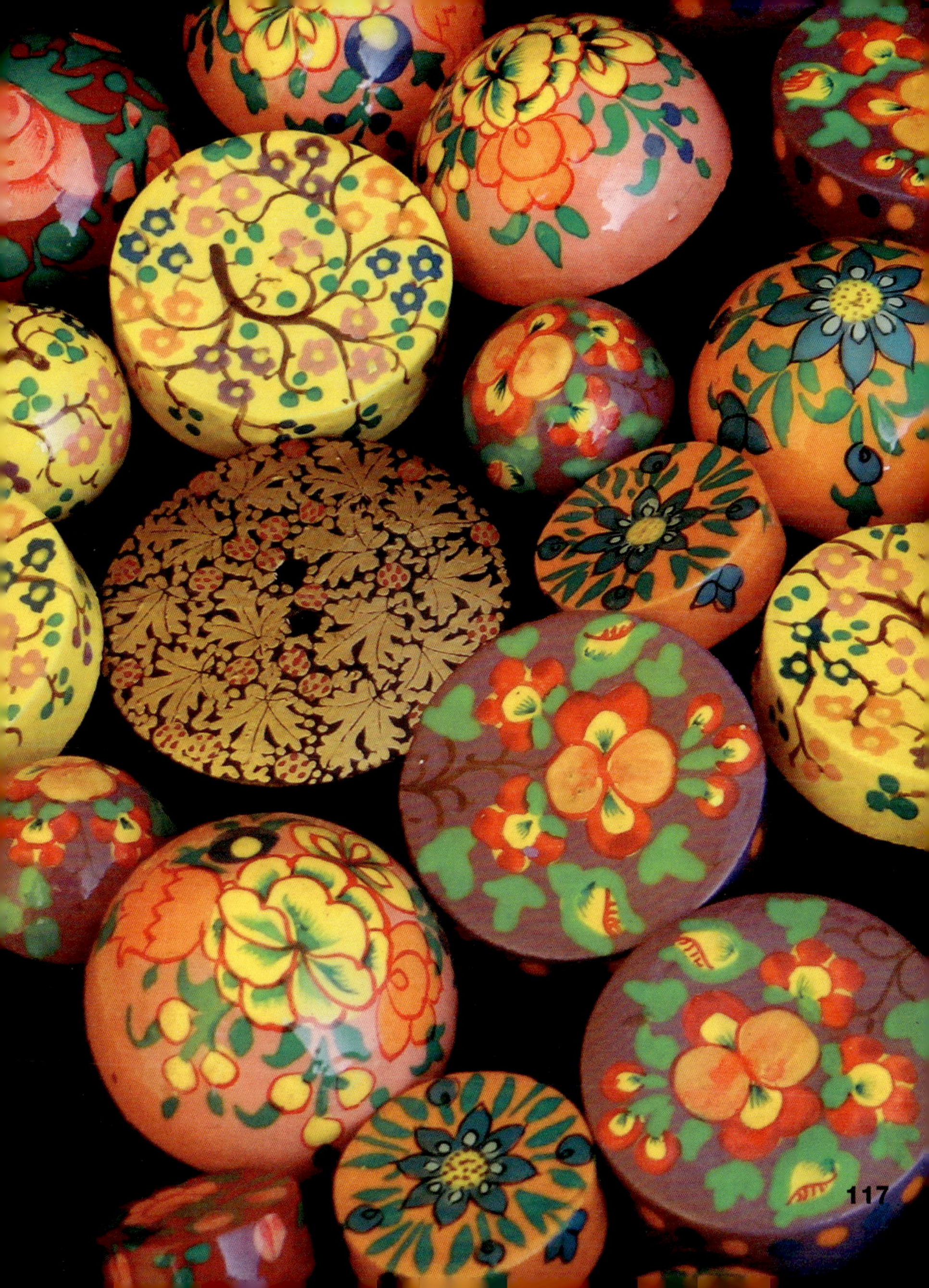

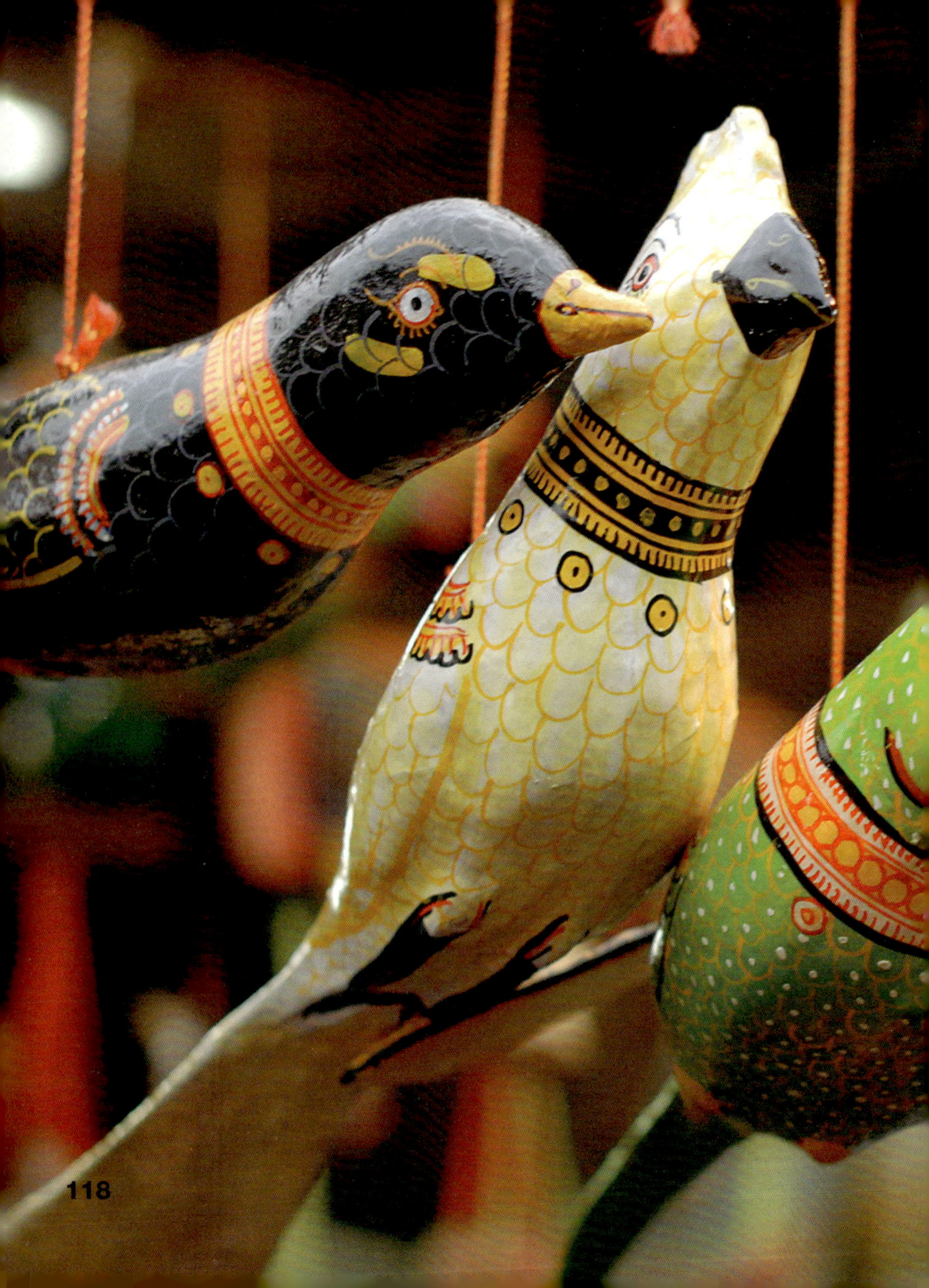

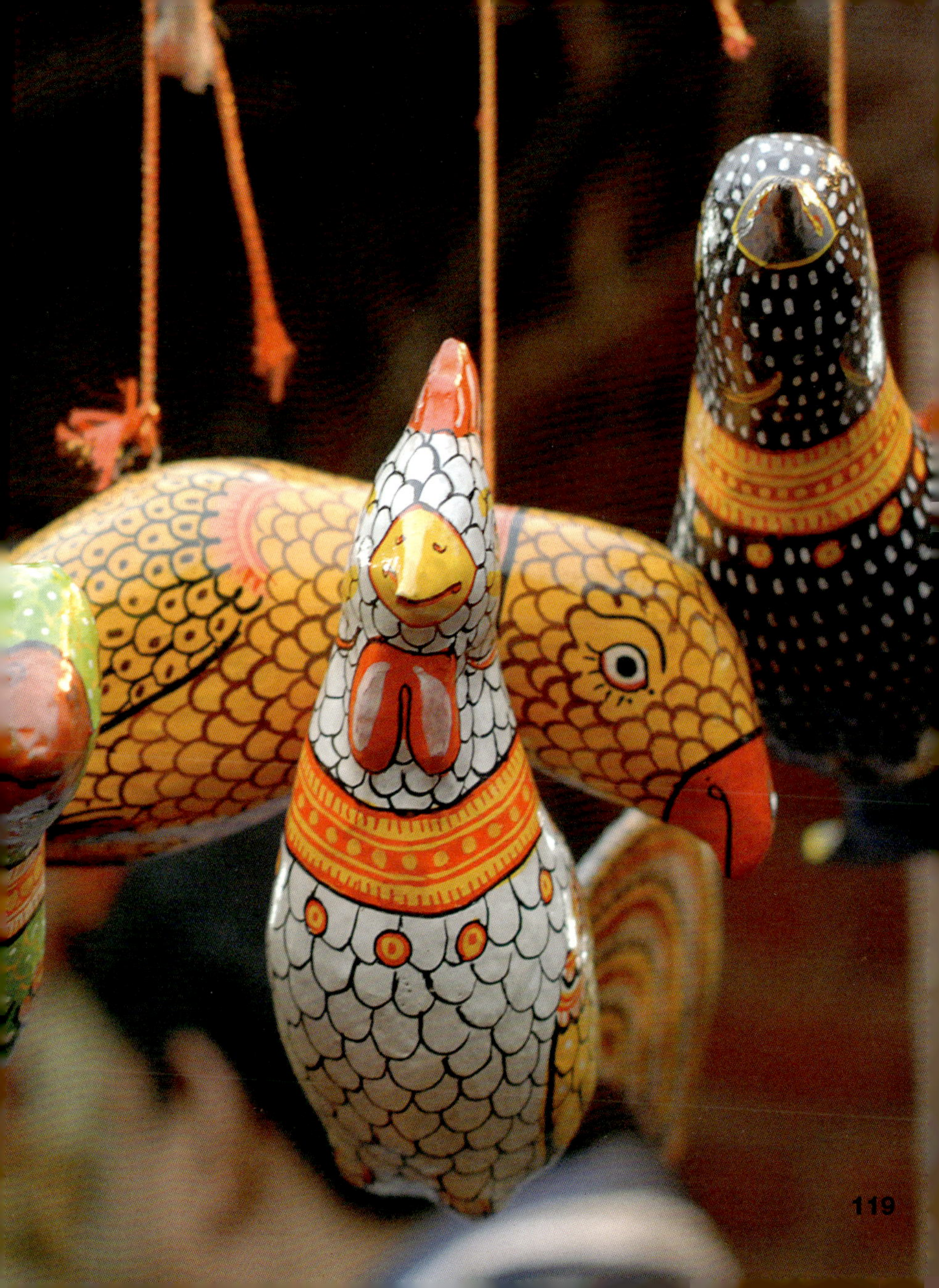

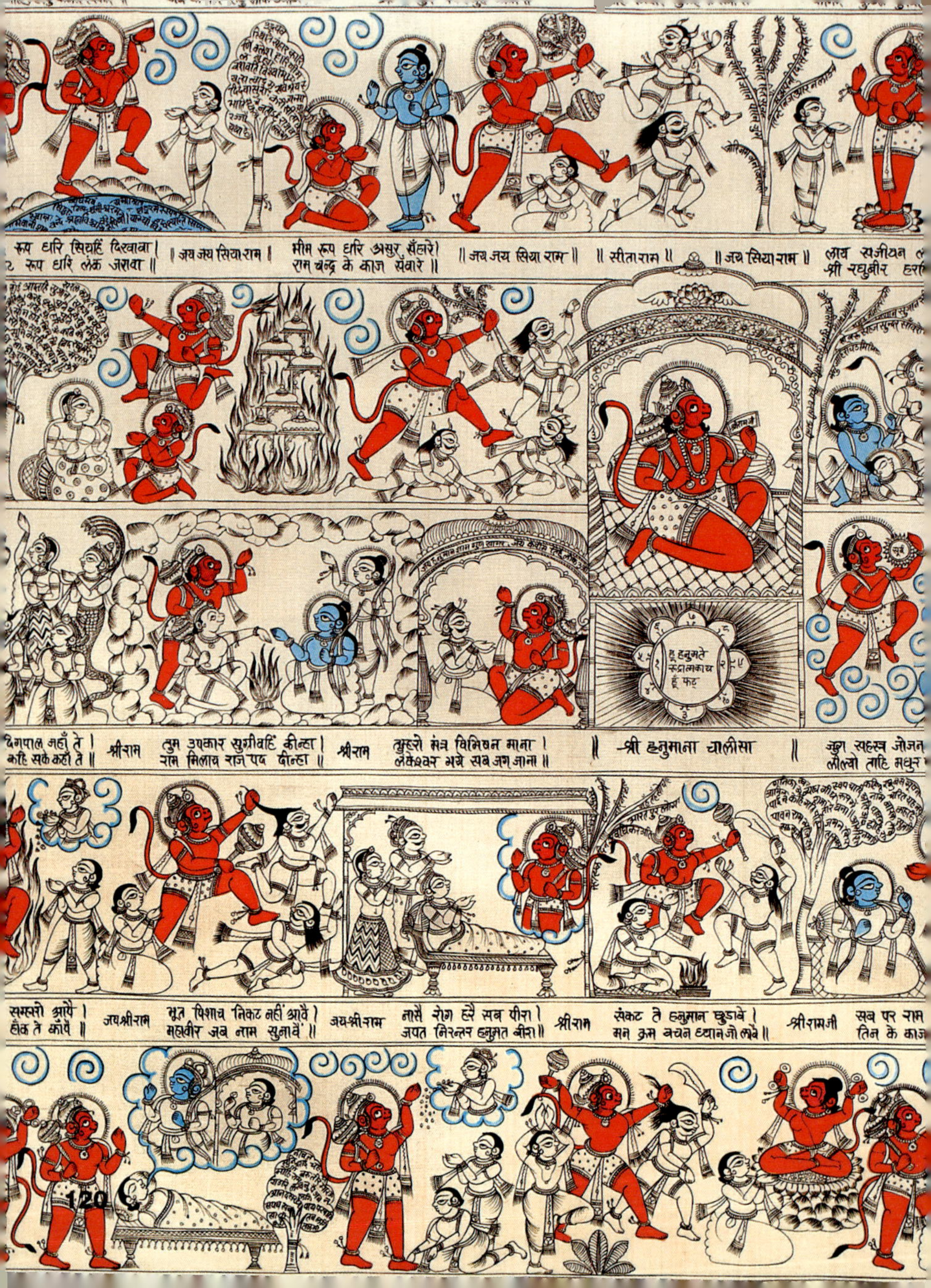
रूप धरि सियहिं दिखावा।
र रूप धरि लंक जरावा॥
॥ जय जय सिया राम ॥
भीम रूप धरि असुर सँहारे।
राम चन्द्र के काज सँवारे॥
॥ जय जय सिया राम ॥
॥ सीताराम ॥
॥ जय सिया राम ॥
लाय सजीवन
श्री रघुबीर हर
दिगपाल जहाँ ते।
कहि सके कहाँ ते॥
श्रीराम
तुम उपकार सुग्रीवहिं कीन्हा।
राम मिलाय राज पद दीन्हा॥
श्रीराम
तुम्हरो मंत्र विभिषन माना।
लंकेश्वर भये सब जग जाना॥
॥ श्री हनुमाना चालीसा ॥
जुग सहस्त्र जोजन
लील्यो ताहि मधुर
सम्हरो आपै।
हाँक ते काँपै॥
जयश्रीराम
भूत पिशाच निकट नहीं आवै।
महावीर जब नाम सुनावैं॥
जयश्रीराम
नासै रोग हरे सब पीरा।
जपत निरन्तर हनुमत बीरा॥
श्रीराम
संकट ते हनुमान छुडावे।
मन क्रम बचन ध्यान जो लावे॥
श्रीरामजी
सब पर राम
तिन के काज

I know no sign more ominous for the future of the Indian civilization, than our utter indifference to social industrial idealism, and the heartless callousness with which we have cast aside the services of those who have built our homes, and clothed and wrought for us in the days we learned to despise our own culture – leaving them to eke out a precarious living by making petty trivialities for tourists, curio-collectors, and for the Anglo-Indian bungalows, or to drift into the ranks of menial labourers or factory hands. Do you think that we can thus degrade the status of so many men without impairing the vitality of our national life and without injuring the basis of its possible prosperity?

~ Ananda K. Coomaraswamy
Art and Swadeshi

Captions

Photo Credits:

Dastkari Haat Samiti

Students of Delhi Public School, Ghaziabad

Drupad

Sunil Kumar

Nayantara Bhandari